PREAC
WHAT WE

MOWBRAY PREACHING SERIES

Series editor: D. W. Cleverley Ford

Preaching on Devotional Occasions: D. W. Cleverley Ford
Preaching on Special Occasions, Vol. 3: Edward H. Patey
More Preaching on Favourite Hymns: Frank Colquhoun
Preaching on Great Themes: D. W. Cleverley Ford
Preaching the Risen Christ: D. W. Cleverley Ford
Preaching the Incarnate Christ: D. W. Cleverley Ford
Preaching for Our Planet: Hugh Montefiore
Preaching on the Crucifixion: D. W. Cleverley Ford
Preaching on the Historical Jesus: D. W. Cleverley Ford
Preaching for All Seasons: John Vipond
Preaching on God's Justice: John B. Taylor
Preaching What We Believe: D. W. Cleverley Ford

Preaching at the Parish Communion:
ASB Epistles – Year One, Volume 2: Dennis Runcorn
ASB Gospels – Year Two, Volume 2: Peter Morris

PREACHING WHAT WE BELIEVE

D. W. CLEVERLEY FORD

MOWBRAY

Mowbray
A Cassell imprint
Wellington House, 125 Strand, London WC2R 0BB
387 Park Avenue South, New York 10016-8810

First published 1995

British Library Cataloguing-in-Publication Data
A catalogue record for this book is available from the British Library.

ISBN 0-264-67363-8

Phototypeset by Intype, London
Printed and bound in Great Britain by
Biddles Ltd, Guildford and King's Lynn

CONTENTS

ACKNOWLEDGEMENTS

I am grateful to Ruth McCurry, Religious Editor of Cassell, the publishers, for suggesting that I write this book with this title, and to Judith Longman, also Religious Editor of Cassell, for seeing it through the publishing process. Also to Miss Barbara Hodge, a former colleague at Lambeth Palace and now retired in one of the flats at Canterbury managed by the Cathedral, who typed the MS.

D. W. CLEVERLEY FORD
Lingfield 1994

INTRODUCTION

A simple and straightforward title for a collection of sermons: 'Preaching what we believe'. But is the matter so simple? What do we believe? What do Christians really believe? What do the Churches believe today? They seem uncertain, divided, if not confused like the age in which we live and this at a time when the mass of people lacks a sense of direction. Coupled with a contempt for authority and the fashion for 'doing one's own thing' the outcome is a sediment of meaninglessness about human existence altogether in the midst of feverish activity. What is to be preached in this situation?

The word 'preaching' in the title is regulative. What is being offered is not a miscellaneous assortment of theological propositions but beliefs *for preaching*. Beliefs there have to be. There cannot be preaching without them. Even so the preacher is not in the pulpit first of all as a teacher, not even of religious truths. He is there to help his hearers manage the complicated task of living today in a complicated and often depressing, puzzling world. This will condition not only what is said but also how it is said. It will also control the selection of subjects chosen for preaching. Only a portion of material is appropriate for preaching when motivated by pastoral concern. And this selection is further governed when what we have in mind is the Christian preacher. Christianity is an historical religion. That is to say it has its roots in historical events even though the preaching is orientated towards contemporary situations both personal and communal. A collection of sermons on 'Preaching what we believe' must therefore be expected to build on the historical events that account for its existence.

Some will see all this as a call for fundamentalism. Fundamentalist preaching is energetic. It appears authoritative and in limited circles can fill churches. Preaching on the other hand which recognizes that there are some matters on which we must remain agnostic, and live with questions, may seem limp, if not lukewarm, and lukewarmness never attracts, it does not build churches. Is there not however a form of *positive preaching* able to make its appeal to the open mind, delivered with warmth and intelligence? The conviction that there is lies behind this collection of sermons entitled 'Preaching what we believe'.

The preacher must believe in what he preaches and not merely assent to it. That is to say it must come from the heart as well as the head. Furthermore preaching is conditioned by what the preacher is. Even more, it is conditioned by what his/her beliefs have made him/her. The preacher is the sermon before any words are spoken either arousing initial attention or dispelling it. The preaching cannot be divorced from the preacher, what he/she is and what he/she is not. This is the terror and the glory of the preaching ministry. The terror is that the preacher may diminish the message; the glory is that the believing quality of the preacher may so shine through that even a technically indifferent sermon may be effective. Preaching what we believe, really believe, is the secret of preaching that moves the hearers.

There has to be at least one indispensable stratum in Christian belief before any Christian preaching is possible: this is belief in Christ. To state this seems obvious. Christian preaching is proclaiming Christ. But does this simply mean testimony to Jesus of Nazareth, his life and his teaching? Does it mean witness to the risen Christ as a spiritual presence now? Does it mean both of these but linked to the historical event of the man Jesus being raised from the dead? We can only preach what we believe, but unless preachers have firm convictions about the resurrection that first Easter Day they will certainly not be in the Apostolic Succession of Christian preaching and they will lack the dynamism that makes for a wholesome Christian faith and one that issues in compassion and practical action.

D.W.C.F.
1994

1

THE PRESENCE OF GOD

God . . . is not far from each one of us, for in him we live and move, in him we exist.

ACTS 17.27 (NEB)

I have been asked to preach a course of sermons under the general title *Preaching What We Believe*. There can be no doubt that this request stems from the feeling that the Church today is not quite sure what it believes. Maybe this is only partly true but in so far as it is, the witness of the Church in the modern world is enfeebled. We cannot preach unless we know what we believe. This is not the same as saying that we cannot preach unless we can supply proofs, scientific proofs, of what we believe. This cannot be. But we can state clearly what we believe and not be ashamed to admit that there are also questions to which we do not know the answers. Call this a measure of agnosticism, if you wish, I shall not dissent from it. Indeed I think preachers are more likely to gain a hearing if they are ready to make this admission. But there are some basics in our beliefs that are not optional. They constitute the bottom line in our preaching. Maybe they need to be handled in a new way if they are to be intelligible in the modern world but they cannot be jettisoned or explained away. Christian preachers must therefore be faithful to the Christian tradition but also alive to the need for re-interpretation. This is not easy but the summons to the preacher lies here.

1 WE BELIEVE IN GOD

We begin then with our first fundamental. We believe in God. But why? Suppose I descended from this pulpit and asked you, each one, why you believe in God what would you say? Yes, I can see you hesitating. After a moment you answer, 'Well, I don't really know. I suppose I believe in God because I was brought up that way. I have never really thought about the reasons. After all, most people believe in God, don't they?, and come to think of it, right round the world, many with religions other than the Christian.' And this is true. The great majority of people do believe in a power beyond themselves. The belief comes naturally to them. It is in fact a human *intuition*. Men and women feel that there is 'Another' out there who has affinity with them. So in times of distress especially, but also in times of gladness, they appeal to this One who cannot therefore be wholly unlike us.

What all this means is that we do not need to make out an elaborate case for believing in God, or offer an apology for believing. To believe in God is natural. It is the unbeliever who has to strain after reasons.

2 THE FUNCTION OF WONDER

But what is it that arouses this belief in God in the first place? I think it is wonder, wonder at the marvellous world of nature all around us. It arises very soon in the development of the human being. It is a characteristic of childhood. Wonder is the soil in which belief in God takes root. This is why children do not find it difficult to believe in God or find it incongruous to talk to him in prayer.

A short while ago I had to visit the doctor in his surgery. No, nothing serious, so I am not appealing for sympathy! You know the routine. I was shown into the waiting room, and that was an appropriate description. I waited, and I became bored with the waiting. The magazines supplied on the table failed to arouse my interest. Then I noticed a small boy aged about six on the other side of the room also waiting with his mother, also bored. All of a sudden his eye lit on an aquarium in the opposite corner. All illuminated it was, with dozens of little fish swimming about in it. He was captivated. He drew closer to it, climbed up on a chair to gain an even closer look, called his mother to watch with him. What caught my attention was not the aquarium, but the boy's eyes, the boy's face, the boy's whole bearing. Wonder was stamped all over him. And I said to myself, if that boy isn't thwarted he will go a long way for he has wonder in him, the root, as Aristotle said, of all wisdom.

3 GOD IS THE REASON FOR OUR EXISTENCE

But how are we to think of God? How are we to represent him in our preaching? When St Paul came to Athens in the course of his missionary tours he saw at once how the Athenians were presenting him. There wasn't a public or conspicuous place in the city which was not specialized by being made to provide a pedestal for a representation in wood or stone of some god or goddess. Paul saw these representations as idols and Athens filled with idols. And the sight shocked him. He said so, and for this reason, that God cannot be represented by any sort of figure, animal or human, mythical or natural. God is like the air we breathe and in default of which we should not even exist. We are alive because of the air. We are alive because of God, and so to assert that there is no God does not make sense. Listen to St Paul speaking, Acts 17.24–28 (NEB): 'The God who created the world and everything in it, and who is Lord of heaven and earth, does not live in shrines made by men . . . for he is himself the universal giver of life and breath and all else . . . he is not far from each one of us, for in him we live and move, in him we exist.'

I want to emphasize the phrase 'for in him we live and move *and in him we exist*'. So in our preaching we shall have to leave behind this all too common stereotype, God as a kind of superman, all-powerful, all-seeing and absolutely unchangeable, set high above the world as we know it, the Creator of everything just as we see it now. This is not what we believe, this is not what we preach. How can we if we are to take evolution seriously?, and we must, though not perhaps too seriously. The 'Big Bang' theory was promulgated by the Belgian astronomer Georges Lemaître that ten thousand million years ago all matter was contained in one primal atom which exploded into millions of fragments, one of which is our solar system; I say not too seriously because it is now being questioned in scientific circles. So we do not preach God as a kind of super Being but as the ground of all being, the source and climate of all existence, ever present and not distant from any one of us.

Is this all too abstract a conception of God for us to take in? Let me give you an illustration. Every summer thousands upon thousands of people make it their aim to be (as they put it) in 'the sun'. They do not address the sun, they do not make any specific request to it, all they seek is to be in its presence, its healing presence, bodily and mentally. They play games in the sun, they swim, they lie about on beaches, active or relaxing, being 'in the sun' is what counts. Likewise the essence of real religion, practical religion is the consciousness of being in the presence of God which is about us all the time, 'closer than our hands and feet' as St Paul said, but of which too often we are so little conscious.

4 THE HEART OF PRAYER

In the light of this perhaps we can understand what is the heart of prayer. It is not first of all asking God for anything, it is making the effort to realize that we are *in his presence*. I said 'making the effort'. I like this little story about the late Archbishop Ramsey of Canterbury. He was asked how long he spent each morning in prayer. 'About two minutes', came the reply, and the questioner was shocked. An Archbishop spending only two minutes in prayer! Then the Archbishop added, after a pause, 'but it takes me about half an hour to get there'. Yes, time and effort are required to realize the presence of God all about us in our busy lives but we have not made contact with the real God unless we come this way.

We need helpers for this and they are available. Perhaps the first is the wonder (note the word) of the natural world. For some of us it is easier to realize the presence of God on a mountain top, or a woodland scene in the autumn with its riot of leaves in reds and browns. But there is also magnificent architecture, and music and literature. All these need to be cherished, some especially for some types of people, others for others. The end point is the same, to realize the presence of God, the God who is all about us, closer than our hands and feet, the very ground of our being, the reason why we exist at all.

5 GOD ACTS IN A PERSONAL WAY

God is not a super person, no, but he acts in a personal way. He loves, he cares, he suffers. He guides people. He forgives their sins, brings them to life eternal. If the Bible does not say all this and more about God it scarcely says anything about him at all. And there are countless people ready to testify to their own spiritual experience of God as a caring presence. Above all he understands us, knowing us even better than we know ourselves. There is nothing about us that lies outside his concern. And because God acts in a personal way we cannot refer to him as *It*. Moreover although we use the personal pronoun *he*, it has nothing to do with gender. *She* would be equally suitable or unsuitable, and he/she does not place God outside gender. Of course there is deep mystery about God, we cannot really comprehend God, but if we could, what we comprehended would not be God. But God has real objective existence, let there be no doubt about this. God is not the projection of our own way of thinking as some try to maintain. This is not what we believe. This is not what we preach. God is the ultimate reality. Without God there is nothing.

* * *

This sermon must close. There has been some difficult abstract thinking in it. This is unavoidable. So let me end on a practical note. Tomorrow morning before you begin your day say to yourself 'God is present with me, close at hand and will be throughout the whole twenty-four hours. Nothing will happen beyond his care and concern. I can enter into this day with confidence. I can lift up my head and I will, so help me God.'

2

THE CHURCH'S BASIC CONFESSION

Simon Peter replied, 'You are the Christ, the Son of the living God.'

MATTHEW 16.16 (RSV)

Today I propose preaching about another fundamental in this series of sermons entitled *Preaching What We Believe*, namely Christ. We believe in Christ and we preach Christ, indeed if we do not we have no place in a Christian pulpit. You ask me, what is preaching? I will tell you, it is proclaiming Christ. This sounds simple enough but the matter is not so simple, which is why I am going to preach this sermon.

1 INTEREST IN JESUS

First I draw your attention to Jesus, Jesus of Nazareth as he is often called and rightly so. There has been an extraordinary outburst of interest in him in the last ten years. Time was, and not so very long ago, when his existence was doubted but nowadays that idea is dead. He would be a brave man who attempted to maintain today that Jesus was no more than a legendary figure, the product of imaginary and wishful thinking. Jesus lived in Galilee and Judaea, his dates can be provided with a degree of certainty – 4 BC–AD 30. Jesus was a real man.

Moreover he was an extraordinary man. Do you think the religious and political authorities of his day would have been hellbent, as they were, on ridding the country of him if he were a wimp or a crank or some kind of religious ranter? On the contrary those who were not captivated by the power of his personality were afraid of him. What was there that a man such as he could not do? Crowds hung upon his words and stood dumbfounded by his actions. Indeed it was difficult to remain neutral in his presence. Either you adored him or you hated him. Either you believed in him or you wrote him off as a dangerous charlatan.

So what is our attitude today? Would I be far wrong to suggest that Jesus is respected as one of the great leaders of thought that have appeared in the long history of mankind, leaving his mark on its course and even significantly altering its direction? Yes, Jesus is listened to and is to some degree applauded but if the question were asked 'Do you believe in Jesus?' there would be a marked hesitancy, this would seem to be going too far. The word 'belief' is the stumbling block and this of course is what concerns us in these sermons *Preaching What We Believe.*

And now let me put this question. Does respect for Jesus of Nazareth as a striking historical figure make a person a Christian? Let me open it out. Does respect for Jesus *in a country* enable that country to be called a Christian country? Undoubtedly the answer is 'Yes'. What however I have to emphasize is that this general respect of appreciation of the historical Jesus, laudable as it is, does not constitute the basis for the *Church*'s existence and it is the Church that we are considering in these sermons – preaching what we believe, what the Church believes.

2 PETER'S GREAT CONFESSION

Now let me draw your attention to one of the key events in the story of Jesus. It is in fact the great turning point and is recorded in the first three gospels, Matthew chapter 16, Mark chapter 8, Luke chapter 9. It is normally labelled as 'The Great Confession at Caesarea Philippi'. Let me quote from Matthew's version.

> Now when Jesus came into the district of Caesarea Philippi, he asked his disciples, 'Who do men say that the Son of man

is?' And they said, 'Some say John the Baptist, others say Elijah, and others Jeremiah or one of the prophets.' He said to them, 'But who do you say that I am?' Simon Peter replied, 'You are the Christ, the Son of the living God.' And Jesus answered him, 'Blessed are you, Simon Bar-Jona! For flesh and blood has not revealed this to you, but my Father who is in heaven. And I tell you, you are Peter, and on this rock I will build my church, and the powers of death shall not prevail against it.' (16.13–18 RSV)

Now many long and learned books have been written about this important passage of Scripture, not least on the matter of the primacy of Peter and the Church of Rome. And there have been disputations in abundance. Let me however cut short and point to one key sentence. When Peter, in the presence of his fellow disciples, all on his own, dared to risk this momentous confession – what a gasp there must have been all round! 'You are the Christ.' Jesus answered: 'You are Peter and on this rock I will build my church, and the powers of death shall not prevail against it.' On what then is the Church built according to the explicit words of Jesus? It is *the confession* that Jesus of Nazareth is the Christ, the Messiah, this is the rock, this is the foundation. So here we have it in black and white: the Church is not built on respect or even admiration for the historical man Jesus, genuine as that may be, it is built on a confession: Jesus is the Christ, the Messiah.

Now Peter was a lone voice at Caesarea Philippi, and his confession remained a lone voice at Caesarea Philippi and no church was founded on it forthwith, but after the resurrection of Jesus and in the light of it, all was changed. The disciples *recognized the Jesus they knew as the Christ*, the Messiah, and went everywhere proclaiming, preaching, what they had dramatically come to believe. So the Church was founded in Jerusalem at Pentecost and churches were established in many cities in the Roman empire and thereafter in places and countries far beyond. They were all founded on what was believed, and what was preached, about Jesus of Nazareth, that he was the Christ, is the Christ, so the Church is grounded and built upon a *confession*. Christians are they who believe that Jesus is the Christ.

Some sixty years ago the custom was widespread among Church people to bow the head at every mention of Jesus in church, especially of course in reciting the Creed. I was a teenager then, attending what would have to be called a 'Low Church', though it preferred to be known as evangelical. We in our Church did not bow the head at the name of Jesus. We wrote off the practice as High Church. I did not know what I thought. In any case I ceased to think about it. Years later however, when I had my first vicarage at the ripe age of twenty-eight my wife and I let two unmarried sisters have the use of the top flat which we did not need. They came to church, somewhat reluctantly I thought, and one of the sisters made a great fuss and show of indignation because she flatly refused, she said, to bow her head at the name of Jesus whether in the Creed or anywhere else because she did not believe that he was anything other than a striking personality; he was certainly not divine. I was worried. What was I to do? I recalled vividly how William Temple, Archbishop of York and later of Canterbury, when attending the church where I was the curate, always and unfailingly bowed his head at the name of Jesus. Obviously it expressed his belief about Jesus. And so in the Creed I bowed my head and have done ever since. I saw that that simple act said something important. The Church is built on the confession that Jesus is the Christ, not only a striking individual.

3 JESUS IS THE SUPREME REVELATION OF GOD

And now something else even more important. Jesus is the supreme revelation of God. This is what we believe, this is what we preach. If the first three gospels, Matthew, Mark and Luke, are called the Synoptic Gospels because they all tell the story of Jesus from the same general point of view, the fourth gospel, John's gospel, interprets that story and this is what it says:

> And the Word became flesh and dwelt among us, full of grace and truth; we have beheld his glory, glory as of the only Son from the Father . . . No one has ever seen God; the only Son, who is in the bosom of the Father, he has made him known. (John 1.14, 18 RSV)

Did you catch the words? 'He has made him known.' Jesus of Nazareth has made God known, in his life, his words and his works, yes in his very being, he was, he is the revelation of God, the supreme revelation, the revelation beyond compare. Perhaps this word 'revelation' needs opening up. Here is a building you have passed a thousand times. You have noticed it, a solid building, a substantial building, but grey and unadorned, nothing in particular to make you want to enter it. And the day came when you had to call. You rang the bell, the door was opened. You almost gasped. What panelling! What furniture! What carpets! What paintings adorning the walls, and what a garden beyond! You could just see it through the windows. And when you got back home you said 'I had no idea there was all that beyond that very ordinary exterior. I was amazed, my visit was *an absolute revelation*. I shall pass that house again as I have in the past but from now on I shall see it quite differently.'

A poor illustration? Open to criticism? Probably, but it throws a little light on that word *revelation*, which we can so easily write off as a theological cliché. It carries the idea of wonder, amazement and the realization that our understanding of what we have seen will never be the same again. So Jesus of Nazareth in his humble peasant's garb in Galilee and Judaea, a one-time carpenter, and no graduate of any learned academy, is actually more than we could ever dream up; he is the supreme revelation of the eternal God. You ask, what is God like? How can we possibly know? How can anyone know? No one has ever or can see God. No, but you 'see' Jesus from the records we have of him in the New Testament gospels. You and I can see now what God is like. This is a staggering statement, but this is what we believe about Jesus. He is the revelation of God beyond compare. This is what we preach.

3

JESUS AS LORD

For what we preach is not ourselves, but Jesus Christ as Lord, with ourselves as your servants for Jesus' sake.

2 CORINTHIANS 4.5 (RSV)

One of the curious facts about life is that when we reach the time to qualify for the Old Age Pension some events in the past, even trivial ones, stand out in memory much more vividly than those which took place only yesterday, and the names of people fall into the same category. So I can hear in mine, when I was about twelve, my French master at school, Mr Brooks, yes, I can even remember his name! say something one day in class about '*our Lord*'. I was puzzled, so puzzled that I looked round to see if other boys were puzzled. Who was he talking about? This was odd because I was brought up in a Christian home, had been a choirboy, and always attended church. The name Jesus was familiar enough, and Christ as a title I knew. Indeed I would happily have spoken of Jesus Christ, but 'our Lord', no, it was foreign to me, it was not part of my vocabulary.

Now in my sermon today I want to point out that to call Jesus Lord is the index of a proper faith in him. A Christian is someone who believes that Jesus is Lord. Jesus as Lord is what we preach. But it does not come easily. It never did come easily. It took time for this conviction about Jesus to grow among his early followers, but in due time to confess that 'Jesus is Lord' became the faith which men and women were ready to die for rather than deny, and they did, in hundreds. I want to spell this out and I shall go on to suggest why it is that the title 'Lord' and 'our Lord' has dropped out of modern thinking.

1 THE WORD 'LORD' – *KURIOS*

First, then, the use of the word 'Lord' in the Greek world in which Christianity was born and grew up. It was a word on everyone's lips in ordinary, everyday life, being equivalent to 'Sir' or 'Monsieur' or 'Herr' in modern speech. It was a title of courtesy or respect, but gradually it came to denote authority, in the home, in the relationship between master and slave, and of a commander in the army. More specifically it became the title of the Roman Emperor, and in the Eastern part of the empire he was known officially as 'lord and god'. So the word 'lord' – *Kurios* in the Greek – spoke loudly of authority. Authority is what is significant.

Now when we turn to the New Testament we find there the same development of this word 'Lord'. When the official in John 4.49 implored Jesus to come and heal his son he said, 'Sir, *Kurie*, come down before my child dies'. There was no theology present in his mind, only respect. The word is therefore only of limited occurrence in the gospels. People did not know who Jesus was although they were impressed by him. After the resurrection that first Easter, however, all this was changed. They saw him then as Lord, Lord of life and death. And so we read in Acts 2.36 of St Peter preaching as follows: 'Let all the house of Israel therefore know assuredly that God has made him both Lord and Christ, this Jesus whom you crucified.' And St Paul wrote to the Corinthians (2 Cor 4.5): 'For what we preach is not ourselves, but Jesus Christ as Lord (*Kurios*), with ourselves as your servants for Jesus' sake.'

We take this lying down, perhaps regretting that the preacher today should feel it necessary to present all this technical material when what concerns us is living in the modern world. But I have to tell you that no Christian or non-Christian in the early days of the Church took this confession of Jesus as Lord lying down. It was the basic confession of every Christian. A Christian was one who dared to stand up and say 'Jesus is

Lord'. The words were an offence against the State and a liability for the individual Christian. Note the content of the confession – '*Jesus* is Lord', not a mythological or other-worldly being but a man who walked about in Galilee and Judaea and was crucified by the command of the Roman Governor, Pontius Pilate, *he is Lord.* It was, it is, a staggering assertion. And when the Emperor came to take the title Lord (*Kurios*), the State pounced on any who refused to use it, counting them as enemies to the unity of the empire. So what were the Christians to do? Every citizen was bound once a year to offer a pinch of incense to the bust of the Emperor with the confession 'Caesar is Lord', after which they could worship what gods they liked. But the Christians refused. Jesus is Lord, not Caesar. And they paid the price. They chose to die for their faith, in the agonies of the cross, the lions' den, the flames, the torture rack.

It is hard for us sitting comfortably in church to grasp the horror of the Christian dilemma and the price that was paid for the belief in Jesus as Lord and for the preaching of it; we use the phrase 'Jesus Christ our Lord' so glibly in our liturgies, but the very heart of the Christian gospel beats here and is safeguarded or jettisoned with this phrase – Jesus is Lord.

2 THE AUTHORITY OF JESUS OF NAZARETH

And now the authority of Jesus of Nazareth of which the people who encountered him in Galilee and Judaea were very conscious. But, and this is the rub, they did not know who he was, he was a puzzle, even an enigma. They were acquainted with his background, his humble village life in backwater Nazareth. They knew his family and the sheer ordinariness of it, and his garb was that of a manual worker, but he himself was extraordinary. He possessed a personal presence. He looked people straight in the face with penetrating eyes and his diction was pointed and elegant. Without thinking, people called him 'Sir'. But who was he? One question above all others made this question burn – his manifest personal authority.

This burst upon the inhabitants of Capernaum in Galilee at the very outset of his public ministry. He was invited to preach one Sabbath in the synagogue. It was startling because in place of the customary boredom with the pulpit the worshippers (I am quoting from Mark 1.22) 'were astonished at his teaching, for he taught them as one who had authority, and not as the scribes'. And not only were his presence and his words astonishing but also his actions. For example, a man in the congregation was so mentally overpowered that he called out 'What have you to do with us, Jesus of Nazareth? Have you come to destroy us?' But Jesus would brook no interference; he was in command. 'Be silent!' he called out and the unnerved man subsided immediately. Small wonder that all in the synagogue were amazed, saying to one another, 'What is this? A new teaching! With authority he commands even the unclean spirits, and they obey him.'

This then is what I am saying: Jesus in the days of his public ministry did not carry and was not accorded the title 'Lord', no one thought of him, much less spoke of him, as 'the Lord Jesus', indicating authority, but the authority was there, obvious to all with eyes to see and ears to hear, heightening the puzzlement as to who he could be.

And so we have to move on to consider his teaching, striking in form as well as in content and all with the same authority. Six times over in the Sermon on the Mount, so called, as we have it in St Matthew's gospel he repeated 'You have heard that it was said, but I say unto you . . .' Did someone in the listening crowd mutter to his neighbour 'Who does he think he is?' After all, Jesus appeared to be putting himself above the sacrosanct ordinances of Moses, Israel's supreme lawgiver. So the teaching of Jesus was authoritative, that is to say he gave principles for action to which his followers should give priority. He did not lay down laws with penalties for disobeying them, he gave principles. But here is the sharp question: are those principles authoritative in today's world? What for instance about the burning question of marriage and divorce? Is what he said on these subjects to be taken seriously? It will be by those who count Jesus as Lord, and by many others who count what he said as basically beneficial for the community as a whole. When we think about these questions the whole subject of the Lordship of Jesus is lifted out of the realm of biblical history and brought disturbingly into the life and conduct of the Christian today. Is Jesus the Lord? Is he our Lord? The issue is a live one.

3 AUTHORITY OUT OF FASHION

But authority is out of fashion in today's world. No one recently has expressed this more forcefully than Dr Sacks, the Chief Rabbi. Let me quote from an article of his in *The Times* newspaper of 3 December 1993 following on the murder by two schoolboys of James Bulger, aged two. 'We have systematically dismantled our structures of authority. Who today has survived our relentless iconoclasm? Politicians, religious leaders, the royal family, have been mercilessly savaged until there is no one left whose word carries moral force. We recognize public faces through their caricatures. They have become figures of fun. In the process we have robbed our children of any credible model of who we would like them to be.'

So authority is out. No one is to tell us what we should think, what we should do. Each individual must 'do his own thing'. There is no such thing as an objective morality, all is relative. It is not possible to say this is right and that is wrong; everything depends on a person's genes, upon the social conditions in which he/she was brought up, upon nationality and colour of skin. Every life style is legitimate and therefore moral judgements are out of the question. What is right is doing no harm to others which in due time becomes simply 'what I feel like doing'. So no authority is recognized anywhere, and there can be no authoritative persons. Put crudely, 'I'm as good as you'.

So where does the authority of Jesus Christ come in? Who is likely to address him as Lord? Is it surprising then that the address on the lips of ordinary Christians, 'our Lord', has dropped out of fashion and that we no longer bow our heads at the name of Jesus? We all go by our Christian names these days, so

Jesus is just Jesus, almost the same as us though exceptional. We shall need to be careful. The Church will need to be careful. If through familiarity we lose the Lordship of Jesus it will not be long before we lose the faith which saves. It is correct to use the bare name of Jesus when we are referring to the historical man of Nazareth but when we are confessing our faith we had better be careful not to allow his full title 'the Lord Jesus Christ' to drop entirely out of usage. What we believe is 'Jesus is Lord'. This is what we preach. Our hope for time and eternity are bound up in that pregnant confession. Let us safeguard it.

4
THE SAVIOUR

'Be not afraid; for behold, I bring you good news of a great joy which will come to all the people; for to you is born this day in the city of David a Saviour, who is Christ the Lord.'

LUKE 2.10–11 (RSV)

In 1993 the nation was deeply stirred by the brutal murder on 12 February of the two-year-old James Bulger by two boys aged eleven. It sparked off a widespread concern, indeed alarm, about how deep among the youth of today is the apparently complete unawareness of any difference between right and wrong; almost a moral vacuum with devastating results. What could be done? This was the question on everyone's lips. Ought the parents to save the situation? Or the schools? Or the law with stiffer penalties? Could the government *save* the situation? Was there anywhere a *saviour*? Could there be?

In the last two centuries BC and the first two centuries AD, that is, at the turn of the millennium, this kind of bewilderment, only far worse, coupled with despair had taken hold of the entire civilized world of that time. As a result there was a great cry in people's hearts for a saviour, someone to lead them out of what they saw as impending catastrophe. And eyes turned to the Emperors of Rome: one after another, each one from Nero to Hadrian was called the saviour, and the god Serapis was named 'the saviour of all men'.

1 JESUS THE SAVIOUR

It was in the middle of this frightened and frightening time that Jesus was born. And he came to be seen as the years went by as the Saviour, indeed no more loved and widespread title has ever been attached to his name. But he was not seen as the Saviour as he lay cradled in that wretchedly humble manger at Bethlehem. How could he be? Though both St Matthew and St Luke in their nativity stories allude to intimations, first to Joseph: 'you shall call his name Jesus for he will *save* his people from their sins'; then to the shepherds in the fields: 'Be not afraid; for behold, I bring you good news of a great joy which will come to all people; for to you is born this day in the city of David a *Saviour*, who is Christ the Lord.' But this is the remarkable fact, and it is a fact, that Jesus was not seen as the Saviour till he had hung torn, bruised and broken on a cross of wood. It is the crucified Jesus who saves. It might be thought that in the light of the astonishing array of healings that he had achieved in Galilee on the sick, blind, deaf and dumb, old and young alike, men, women and children, he would have been hailed as the Saviour then, especially when I tell you, as I must, that the word in the Greek for these healings is 'save'; he *saved* these people. But no, he was called Teacher or Rabbi but not 'the Saviour' till after he had hung crucified on that ugly little hill outside Jerusalem; it had to be outside the Holy City (so called) because a crucified man was counted as the offscouring of the earth. I tell you, I tell myself yet once again, we have not even begun to appreciate what it means to call Jesus the Saviour until we see him in this horrible situation. There is a pregnant statement which runs like this: 'Jesus reigns from the tree.' Though not diverging from its truth, I would like to change one word: Jesus *saves* from the tree.

An experience I had as long ago as 1930 has remained vivid in my mind; it was a visit to the war cemeteries in Belgium. Thousands and thousands of graves almost as far as the eye could see – graves. Death dominated the landscape but this is what struck me: over each grave was a cross, symbol of salvation. I had never seen so many graves, never seen so many crosses. The scene cried aloud to me the message of the Christian gospel. We have a Saviour. No matter what sins we have committed, and wars are stacked high with sins, terrible sins and sufferings piled all around them, forgiveness and restoration is there for us to grasp in Jesus the crucified, if we in sorrow and penitence do but turn to him. Jesus is the Saviour, the world's Saviour, your Saviour and mine too, the preacher.

Jesus paid for this, paid the price of our forgiveness, paid the price of being the Saviour. Forgiveness is a costly business. When someone has done us a grievous wrong, it 'takes some doing' to forgive. It cannot be done out of anger. It cannot be done out of a demand for rights. It cannot be done while resentment burns. Only love can forgive, nothing else. When therefore Jesus paid the price of our forgiveness, forgiveness for the wrongs we have committed against God and our fellow men and women, the price he paid was the price of love. I must stress this. Jesus was not diverting the anger of God against us sinners by his sufferings on the Cross. God is a God of love. God is a forgiving God and Jesus' mission in this world was to show in his person what God is like, to show us God the Saviour.

2 A SAVED PEOPLE

Now because Christ is the Saviour especially of those who believe in him, Christians are a saved people. It may be that we fight shy of this description. It sounds presumptuous, even overtly pious. Anglicans especially, like me, shy off this. It may even be that we have been accosted by some enthusiastic evangelist, buttonholed and asked 'Are you saved?' Which reminds me of a story I heard of a theological professor in mufti crossing the Atlantic. There was one such enthusiastic evangelist on board, possibly American, unknown to the professor but whom he discovered when the evangelist engaging him in conversation put his direct question 'Are you saved?' But the professor's reply floored him. 'Do you mean' – and he used the Greek word for 'saved' in the *past* tense? – 'or do you mean' – and he used the Greek word for 'being saved' in the *present* tense? – 'or do you mean will be saved in the future', and he used a corresponding word in the *future* tense. Not surprisingly the 'hot gospel' evangelist bolted. Was the professor unkind to answer in this fashion? Possibly, but what he said was correct. Salvation is a comprehensive experience. Certainly we have been saved by the cross of Christ. As we have responded we have received the forgiveness of our past sins, but what about the present? What about the sins we commit today, tomorrow and the day after, sins of omission as well as of commission? That occasion when we could have visited that broken-hearted man next door but it interfered with the television programme we wished to watch? We have been saved by the Cross of Christ but we are only being saved in so far as we follow in the steps of the Jesus of whom we read in the gospels. And what about the closing of the last chapter of our lives, what happens then? Shall we be saved? What has the resurrection of Christ on Easter Day to say about this? So the answer to the question 'Are you saved?' – and make no mistake, it is a proper question – is 'Yes, No and Not yet'. We cannot therefore be presumptuous but we can be quietly confident because Jesus is the Saviour and the salvation he offers us is not based on our merit but on his love, whatever mess we may have made of things. This is the good news, this is the Christian gospel. Because of Christ, the Saviour, Christians dare to think of themselves as a saved people.

3 THE SAVIOUR FROM ETERNAL DEATH

And now Jesus as the Saviour from eternal death. Not many people would admit it but as the years go by and strength begins not only to lessen but to fail, the thought of death begins to nag. What comes next when we draw our final breath? Is there a life to come?

It is true that since the dawn of history there has existed a belief in a life beyond the grave, but hazy, problematical and fearsome. Jesus saved from this. The writer of the Second Letter to Timothy in the New Testament pointedly called Jesus our Saviour and proceeded with this firm affirmation, 'he has broken the power of death and brought life and immortality to light through the Gospel' (1.10 NEB).

And this salvation from eternal death includes salvation of the body. Listen to this from St Paul's letter to the Philippians (3.21 NEB): 'He will transfigure' (note the word) 'He will transfigure the body belonging to our humble state, and give it a form like that of his own resplendent body, by the very power which enables him to make all things subject to himself.' So in the life to come our personality and individuality will remain and that of those we love will also remain. We shall be recognizably ourselves. We shall not be absorbed into the divine, mystically swallowed up. We shall have our bodies, not the bodies we have now, though not without relationship to them. So we shall express our individualities through our transfigured bodies as we do now – through our bodies of humble estate. There have been religions which have viewed death as a release from the body, considering it to be the source of evil, temptation and sin. Not so the Christian gospel. Did not Jesus reveal the very nature of God *in a human body*? We respect the body then and we believe on the strength of the gospel that every part of us will be saved, no, not as it is now but transfigured, or transformed, as is the shrivelled bulb in the winter garden with the coming of spring, it becomes a glorious flower.

This is the Easter gospel. Jesus saves for the life to come. He saves because he himself rose triumphant over death, triumphant not only for himself but for us. By him we are saved from eternal death. We have a Saviour unto eternal life.

Before I close, may I say this as a preacher who is also a pastor? I may be addressing someone who has been through the blackness of a recent bereavement. You cannot forget the closing of those curtains at the crematorium. My friend, I know. Let the light of the Christian gospel shine upon you. We and those we love are not lost in an eternal death. Jesus is the Saviour, the Saviour of us all and of each in our distinctiveness. Hold on to this. I will hold on to it too.

5
GOD WITH US

Behold, a virgin shall conceive and bear a son, and his name shall be called Emmanuel (which means, God with us).

MATTHEW 1.23 (RSV)

Well! There you have it, straight from the shoulder! 'A virgin shall conceive and bear a son.' But she can't, can she? No girl can become pregnant without male insemination. But the Creed we recite in Church, enunciating what we believe, does not give way; 'born of the Virgin Mary', we repeat Sunday by Sunday. Or if you reckon it sounds less uneducated in the Latin tongue, *natus ex Maria Virgine*, but it doesn't really help. What we are up against is scientific, even common-sense impossibility, and if this is where the Christian religion is based, the whole edifice is reckoned by some to be decidedly shaky and is perhaps best left to topple down.

1 ST MATTHEW'S STORY

Now I could proceed with comments on religion and science and we might perhaps be wiser, I don't know. In any case I will say something along this line in a moment. First however, note how the New Testament opens at St Matthew's gospel. There is nothing like a scientific approach, instead a very human story told with feeling and replete with misunderstanding, bewilderment and pain. There is no immediate joy here. It is about Joseph in love with Mary, a village girl, and engaged to her. He had no eyes for anyone but Mary, she was all the world to him. Do you know what this means? I do. Love is at the front, back and sides of this human relationship. And then, just when Joseph was about to complete the engagement in marriage Mary was found to be with child, and not by him! Put yourself in Joseph's shoes! Can you?

Yes, I am starting by lifting the whole subject of the Virgin birth out of the realm of academic scientific discussion and putting it back where the New Testament in St Matthew's gospel firmly places it, a desperate human predicament of two good people. Mary had to tell Joseph she was pregnant. What else could she do? There must have been tears, many tears. Did she say to Joseph, 'This is God's child'? And did Joseph believe her? Would you have believed her? Poor Joseph! Poor Mary!

Matrimonial troubles are common these days and where at the root there is tension between law and love, the pain is sharp. So here. Joseph felt he must break with Mary. But the very thought hurt terribly. He loved Mary. And she, Mary, could not think of life without Joseph. But over them both hung the fact that in Palestine at this time an engagement was legally binding and could only be broken by a writ of divorcement which meant publicity. Joseph shrank from this and because he so loved Mary decided to put her away on the quiet. She must slip back home to Nazareth. There would be gossip of course, but better that than a public scandal. And while the anguish burned in Joseph's soul and he could not believe that Mary had known some man carnally, not Mary, surely not Mary! God spoke to him in a dream: 'Do not fear to take Mary your wife, for that which is conceived in her is of the Holy Spirit.' And he believed and married Mary as she was, and the child was born. Then this: Joseph gave the child a name, yes Joseph! He called him Jesus.

Now you are at liberty to rub out this whole story, you can write 'Rubbish' across it or, less crudely perhaps, a 'moving story' but at best 'a pious legend'. In that ancient world stories about virgin births were two a penny. Pythagoras, Plato, Caesar Augustus were all said to have been born miraculously of virgins. But that was in the Hellenistic, the Greek world. This story in the New Testament bears no mark of a Greek origin whatsoever, it is thoroughly Hebrew. Moreover it is quite out of the ordinary in telling of a virgin belonging to the humbler classes. I said just now, you can write off this nativity story if you like, and, I dare to add, still be a Christian, but I warn you. You have not rid yourself of all the difficulties. For one thing, if Jesus really was the child of Joseph and Mary then he came into the world through the will of Joseph and perhaps of Mary too, or Jesus was simply the product of a sexual urge, the will and purpose of God was not responsible, not directly anyway. But the Biblical message is that something entirely new happened with this birth, something epoch-making. God of his own will and purpose for the saving of mankind came there and then into our world where we are and how we are. So my text from Matthew 1.23: 'Behold, a virgin shall conceive and bear a son, and his name shall be called Emmanuel (which means, God with us).' This is the essential message of Christmas, this is the root of the Christian religion. The Word of God became flesh, God in human form on earth, the Incarnation. Now if this is true – and I admit, it takes some believing, God on this earth in the form of a man – is it surprising if the manner of this extraordinary (I almost want to say fantastic) event was initiated in an extraordinary way, a virginal conception? Could it not be congruous?

2 SCIENCE AND ULTIMATE REALITY

Nevertheless we shall have to concede that the nativity story of how Jesus came to be born is not scientifically verifiable, but this raises a further question – are we sure that reality can only be grasped by means of scientific verification? Granted, it was not long since this idea was widely held. The universe was confidently taken to be like a giant clock whose mechanism was regular, constant and wholly in control. So miracles cannot possibly happen, variations from the norm are out of the question, the clock must be unvarying. And let us be clear: if the universe did not for the most part perform in this fashion how could life proceed? The case of gravitation is an obvious case in point. The most up-to-date science however says something different. It proclaims a random element in the working of the universe, chance even plays a part. Furthermore quantum physics says that events are altered by being observed. The world is a flux and only has the appearance of being fixed and orderly by our seeing it so. Science, then, though important and a worthy pursuit of man, is not the *infallible* road to our knowledge of reality. All this is why we shall be wise not without more ado to write off the nativity story as unscientific, and because the heart of the story tells of *God* coming into this world we had better be doubly careful. There is mystery here beyond what science can tell us.

3 GOD HAS COME WHERE WE ARE

Now let me reassume my proper role which is that of a preacher concerned with life now, its ups and downs, its joys and sorrows, its successes and its failures and what lies on the other side of death. What gospel, what good news, if any, has Christmas to give us to make our hearts glad? The answer is, God is where we are and how we are, closer than our hands and feet, always accessible, ever ready to hear us when we cry out to him in our need. And this is the remarkable fact, the world over, people of all races, customs and cultures do this. There is no nation anywhere completely bereft of some religion, nor ever has been. Man's feeling after God is part of him. The need for a Transcendent Being out beyond us, yet like us, and therefore approachable, is constant. Why is this? Surely it can only be because *God is the Ultimate Reality*. And this is what Christmas says. This God is not far off. He has come close to us that we may know him and be lifted up by his presence, first in the infant Jesus cradled in a manger and then in his life and ministry, crowned with his crucifixion and resurrection. The truth is we are slow to recognize him.

Let me pinpoint this with a story, not mine, it comes from a German writer called Mayer Skumenz. It is about a man who lived on his own in a house with no one to help him. One day he received a message to say that he was to receive a visitor. The news nearly frightened him out of his wits. It was months if not more since he had taken even a duster to the place; it was filthy, cobwebs abounded. Nearly mad with desperation at the very thought of a visitor, he went out into the street and cried aloud 'Will no one come to help me clear up this filthy place? I am expecting a visitor any day and I must have it tidied up.' And a man appeared and said 'I will' and set about forthwith making the house clean and acceptable. The two of them worked at it the whole day through. When evening came the householder looking around his transformed house said to the helper 'Well, now we can sit at the table and wait for my visitor'. 'No need', said the volunteer cleaner, '*I am the visitor.* I have been here all day, let us eat and be at peace.'

So God, to cleanse us from all that spoils what we might be, came where we are, came as the Babe of Bethlehem and the carpenter of Nazareth. He got dirty, for they nailed him to a cross. This is the Christmas message. This is what we believe. This is what we preach. Tell me, if you wish, that this story is not verifiable, it is unscientific. But my message today as a Christian preacher is this. There are wonders and there are mysteries beyond what can be proved scientifically and one of them is the birth of Jesus. We shall be wise to grasp this with both hands, for in it is eternal life. God has come where we are. Hear the text again from St Matthew, chapter 1, verse 23.

> Behold, a virgin shall conceive and bear a son, and his name shall be called Emmanuel (which means, God with us).

6
THE INCARNATION

And the Word was made flesh, and dwelt among us.
JOHN 1.14

One of my memories is a church service I attended with my wife. We sat together in the back seat of the nave. As we came away, walking through the churchyard, we each mentioned the sermon, agreeing that it was 'a good one'. The preacher held our attention; more than that, there was a message for us, we heard God speaking through the words of the sermon. Each of us was inwardly moved. As we walked I mentioned in passing the apt illustration the preacher had employed to light up his theme. My wife agreed but I saw a smile on her face, quite kindly, but a smile. Then she said 'Pity he didn't get his facts right'. Now my wife could outclass me in history any day, so I kept quiet on this except to say 'But we heard a word from God this morning, didn't we?' Warmly she agreed, the historical *faux pas* not withstanding.

1 THE QUESTION OF HISTORICAL ACCURACY

I thought about this when we reached home and we talked again. The Bible stories are a kind of sermon. Their aim is to convey the word of God. In them, and through them, we hear God speaking to us. Most frequently the stories tell of historical events, they are not fables or fairy stories. And they are presented in an arresting fashion with due attention to literary style. But are they *historically* accurate? This question worries some people greatly. And the answer is, yes, in general they are, but in every detail, no, even the ordinary reader cannot fail to notice how in places where two accounts of the same event are given they do not always tally exactly. So must we write the Bible off? Some people do. But does not the Word of God come over to us through the stories just as it did in that sermon my wife and I heard when the preacher apparently did not get all his facts right?

Last Christmas through the media the nativity stories heard over and over again at carol services were frequently passed off as legends and not as historical accounts of anything that actually happened. The story of the wise men following a star in particular was dismissed in this fashion. Maybe it is unhistorical, even though the period in which the story is set was one of widespread hope of some sort of Messiah appearing, and the study of the stars for guidance was rife. So perhaps the story is possible, even probable historically, though most of us would boggle at the star locating the actual place where the Christ child was to be found. This however is the point I want to make. What we believe at Christmas and what we preach is not dependent on the historicity of the wise men or the star of Bethlehem (so called). After all, two of the four gospels, St Mark and St John, do not even mention the nativity stories. We can be good Christians even though we put a big query over their historicity. What we must not do however is to write off the Bible because here and there are historical inaccuracies. With my wife that Sunday we heard the word of God in spite of the preacher's historical *faux pas*. The Bible is not first and foremost a history book. It has another aim than to record past events. Its purpose is to inspire, yes, inspire faith in the living God. This is what we believe. This is why we preach from it.

So do not at Christmas ever think of rubbing out the old and well-loved nativity stories, the shepherds in the fields and the wise men following a star. Listen instead to what they are saying. They are saying something stupendous, something which indeed takes some believing but without which they are little else but decoration. They are saying that God has come where we are, he has come on to our side where there is beauty and where there is muck. Apparently no place is too filthy, too humble, nor even too sophisticated where God has not come and will not come. And now in Jesus 'the Word made flesh', as our text puts it, we can 'see' God, we can know God and we can, through believing in him, be lifted up and transformed. This is the good news of Christmas – the incarnation, the new start in creation, God in Christ for us. This is what we believe, this is what we preach.

2 THE NEW BEGINNING

Let me expand on this. We believe that the coming of Jesus into the world was/is the new creation, the new beginning, the new start. All that exists of course has its origin in God, this is basic to our belief in God. The Bible stamps it on the minds of its readers with its clear-cut opening words 'In the beginning God created the heavens and the earth'. Now note this: when the writer of St John's gospel set about introducing the coming of Jesus into the world he did not tell of the shepherds in the fields and the wise men following a star (which is not to say he was unacquainted with these stories or disbelieved them). No, he had a larger purpose on hand, it was to connect that coming with the original creation. So he wrote 'In the beginning was the Word, and the Word was with God, and the Word was God. The same was in the beginning with God. All things were made by him; and without him was not anything made that was made.' So far so good, but then, this astonishing statement: 'And the Word was made flesh, and dwelt among us.' It is astonishing. The coming of Jesus as the babe of Bethlehem and the man of Galilee is declared to be the new beginning, the new genesis, the new creation. God expressing himself (that is the Word of God) in a life able to be seen, even touched. Hear the words again, 'And the Word was made flesh, and dwelt among us'.

This, I repeat, is astonishing, some would say shocking. Perhaps it is: God coming to know his creation *from the inside*. 'He dwelt among us', the meaning of the world disclosed not in abstruse philosophies but in a human life at a particular time, dated by a not very impressive Roman governor of Palestine – Pontius Pilate. God came over to our side, identifying himself with what is indeed God's creation but now fallen, estranged from its creator. We know it as a world of darkness as well as of light, a world of horror as well as nobility, a world where the current Balkan savagery is all too common a feature around the globe. It is to this world that God came at that first Christmas where the muck is thick and the cruelty widespread. 'The Word was made flesh, *and dwelt among us*.' Yes, the kind of world where marriages break up, and children get neglected, and people live in cardboard boxes on the streets of London and thousands upon thousands die of starvation in the Sudan while there are food mountains in Europe. This is the world to which Jesus came in order that there might be a new creation, a new beginning if only we would heed his coming and not ignore it even at Christmas.

3 HUMAN NATURE VALUED

All this is true but there is something else just as astonishing: God by coming to dwell among us obviously accounted human nature as *able* to bear the divine image and live a life that is well-pleasing to God. I say this is astonishing, for who is there among us who, seeing what is going on in the world's frightening trouble spots, does not despair of human nature, especially when one peace conference after another ends in failure? We want to write off the human race as a hopeless disaster. But God does not. He took *human flesh* to reveal the very highest in life and in circumstances where hate assailed him at every turn.

So God entered into the whole range of human experiences including its physical pain and mental anguish. He knew how it felt to be forsaken by those he loved and who he thought loved him. He tasted loneliness, contradiction, mockery and scorn. Not that he knew every kind of pain, no man can, and Jesus was a real man, but he knew in experience the whole range of human suffering. This was involved in the Lord becoming flesh and dwelling among us.

And here we touch on what sets Christianity apart among the religions of the world. *God suffered pain* we human beings inflicted upon him and he did not hit back. On the contrary he forgave his persecutors and he still forgives his persecutors who repent of their misdeeds, and they become new men and women. This is where the new creation God in Christ came to initiate and to fulfil begins, the place of grace and forgiveness.

⋆ ⋆ ⋆

Come back now to where I began this sermon: 'the shepherds out in the fields, keeping watch through the night over their flock' (Luke 2.8 NEB), and the wise men (NEB 'astrologers') from the east come to Jerusalem seeking one born to be the King of the Jews, having observed the rising of his star (Matthew 2.2 NEB). If we cannot accept the nativity stories as accurate records of historical events they nevertheless illustrate vividly the kind of world in which 'the Word was made flesh', and so successfully that they have never failed to capture the imagination of generation after generation of all ages, including children, especially children, who have encountered them. There is the peaceful pastoral scene of shepherds out in the fields keeping watch through the night over their flock; but they were there not only to tend the sheep but to guard them from dangerous thieves. There is the story of the wise men bringing their gifts; it is attractive but it ends with the account of King Herod ordering the massacre of all children in Bethlehem of the age of two years or less. We hardly need to be told how Bethlehem was a place of tears and inconsolable lamentation. And Joseph and Mary had to take to the roads as refugees, Bethlehem quitted for ever. No, do not rub out the colourful nativity stories; hold them in one hand and in the other St John's theological presentation of the Word become flesh, then you will grasp what it cost for God to come into our world to initiate the new creation, the new beginning. It was a rough world he came to save, but he did it, he did it for our sakes. So let the bells ring out at Christmas, let the carols be sung, let the stupendous fact of Jesus' coming be heralded far and wide. We have a Saviour who risked all for us. Surely we cannot hold back from expressing our heartfelt thanks and praise.

7
THE MIRACLES OF JESUS

Who then is this, that even wind and sea obey him?
MARK 4.41 (RSV)

Every morning tens of thousands of people listen to the weather forecasts on the radio and a summary of the daily news which follows. In between, quite often there is a brief warning about a road blockage somewhere. The cause may be a lorry that has shed its load (what a mess this must be!), or a burst water main, or a 'pile up', so called, the result of a car accident. Anyway, whatever the reason, there is a warning of no way through; there is an impassable blockage.

Now in my sermon today I am going to draw your attention to what for some people, perhaps many people, is a blockage to their continuing to go along with the Christian faith, they come up to it and feel obliged to turn back. I refer to the miracles of Jesus. How in our scientific world today can we accept the stories in the gospels about these? The temptation then for the modern preacher is to avoid the issue and to get on with something straightforward like helping our neighbours, but the temptation should be resisted. When something troubles us, say a physical illness or sore, the worst possible attitude is to neglect it. So with the problem of the miracles of the Bible. Yes, there is a problem and they do act as a blockage for some people, sincere people. The preacher therefore, if he is a concerned pastor, must help his hearers, if he can, at this point.

1 THE PROBLEM

What is the problem? I hardly need to spell it out. We live in a scientific and technological age. We look for causes and effects in life all around us and if we are puzzled about something we go on investigating expecting in the end to come up with an answer. Science has led us to think of the universe as a rational structure and our duty is to find out the laws which govern it and then act accordingly. If it did not proceed in this orderly fashion, for example if gravitation did not always work but sometimes when articles were dropped they did not fall to the floor but sailed up to the ceiling, how could we proceed with normal living? Stories about miracles therefore cannot be accepted as factual, they are unscientific.

Strange as it may sound, this is less of a problem now than it was in the eighteenth and nineteenth centuries. That was the age when the discovery of evolution put paid to the older and time-honoured belief that everything in the world was just as God had willed and created it. The principle of natural selection showed on the contrary how forms of life develop and are shaped in reaction to their environment, and all the development is according to unvarying and consistent laws of behaviour able to be studied and catalogued scientifically. And if there is a God he created the world as an interlocking mechanism, and set it going to work, as it were on its own. He did not interfere. It is not surprising therefore that the concept of miraculous intervention into the running of the world was exceedingly suspect. This, as I said, was in the eighteenth and nineteenth centuries. It was called the age of Enlightenment. It would be unfair to assert that the concept of miracles was ruled out altogether but miracles were thought to be so unlikely as not to be worthy of serious attention. Twentieth-century science has, however, moved away from this fixity in the universe. Quantum physics speaks of a principle of indeterminacy and of a random element. We cannot know what will happen in all circumstances.

A greater degree of humility therefore exists among scientists than formerly. This does not mean the problem of miracles in the Bible has gone away. What it does point to is a greater degree of openness, not least on the part of some scientists to try and understand them.

2 THE CATEGORIES OF MIRACLES IN THE GOSPELS

It is time for me to be more specific in speaking about the miracles in the gospels. First of all there are the healing miracles, such as Jesus curing a man with a withered arm, a deaf mute or a case of paralysis. Perhaps we can accommodate these in our thinking nowadays without too much difficulty. Psychosomatic medicine has shown us how interlocking are mind and body in the human frame. Illnesses and inhibitions once reckoned to have a physical cause may now be seen to originate in the mind. And there has grown up a recognition of the healing powers which some strong personalities possess and exercise in these cases. Jesus was an exceptionally strong personality, the intense way in which he looked at people was in itself sufficient indication of this. The sick folk he encountered in Galilee and Judaea, mostly humble and uneducated, would know nothing of these subtleties about the human frame. They would have no better word for the healing that had come to them through the hands or words of Jesus than 'miracle'. We can accept then that these healing miracles, so called, did take place.

But then there are the nature miracles, so called. Three stand out: the turning of water into wine, gallons of it; the stilling of the storm on the Galilean lake; and the feeding of five thousand people with five loaves and two fish. Manifestly our knowledge of psychosomatic medicine does not help at all. Water cannot be changed into wine in the course of a meal. Storms and raging water cannot be quelled by the use of words of command. Matter, be it loaves or fish, cannot be created or for that matter be destroyed, so we were taught in a first lesson in chemistry.

So how shall we accommodate ourselves to these miracles? By rationalizing them perhaps. The turning of the purification water standing at the wedding feast in Cana of Galilee into wine is an allegory of the richness of the Christian gospel replacing the purification rites of the Jewish religion. The stilling of the storm happened because the boat carrying Jesus and his disciples drifted round a headland into slack water out of danger. The feeding of the five thousand took place because when the boy with his five loaves and two fish shared it with someone nearby at Jesus' instigation, everyone else in the great crowd with food tucked away was inspired to do likewise and so all five thousand were fed. The miracle was people being willing to share what they possessed. It has to be said that none of these explanations is really convincing. They have removed the miracles and, if not exactly making the events commonplace, certainly left them with very little if anything to explain.

And so we pass to the third group of miracles, two in fact which are so embedded in the story of Jesus that it is hard, if not impossible, to explain them away. This is, in one sense, true of all the miracles of Jesus. They are an integral part of the narrative, to take them out and keep the whole is like trying to manage an umbrella without a frame. But to return to the two great miracles: they are the virginal conception of Jesus and his resurrection from the tomb on Easter Day. Perhaps it is possible to accept the Incarnation, that is the Word of God become flesh and known as Jesus of Nazareth, without being tied to the idea of a virgin birth. After all, a girl cannot become pregnant on her own. The miraculous nativity stories in St Matthew's and St Luke's gospels, it is suggested, should therefore be read symbolically, they are a *pictorial way* of saying that Jesus was not indeed a man as other men are, he was unique, he was God in human form.

Some Christians are satisfied with this interpretation but what is to be done about the resurrection of Jesus from the grave? The Christian gospel depends on this. Without it, it is difficult to see how Christian preaching really has a message which could be called news, good news. Of course all manner of arguments have been and are addressed to explain away the resurrection, too many to mention here, such as: the tomb was not empty on Easter morning and the appearances of the risen Christ were hallucinations. Never was an event so subject to scrutiny but the wonder is, I was going to say the miracle is, the resurrection of Jesus has withstood all the onslaught against it. This is a fact which ought to make us cautious about rejecting the miraculous element in the ministry of Jesus as a whole. Miracles apparently are an integral part of his story.

3 THE MIRACLES ARE SIGNS NOT STUNTS

And now a third point, and for that matter my last point in this sermon on the miracles of Jesus. They were not stunts. They were not carried out (if they were and I believe they were, most of them anyway) to overpower people's minds with astonishment so that they were willing to believe anything. There is a story at the beginning of Jesus' ministry, before he actually began, when he was tempted to throw himself down from a pinnacle of the Temple and walk away unharmed. Of course crowds would have flocked to such a wonder-worker but he refused it. This was not his way. And on the cross at the end his accusers taunted him with the offer, 'Come down now from the cross and we will believe you'. But he did not. No, the miracles of Jesus were not stunts. They were what St John in his gospel called signs, signs of who Jesus really was. You may remember that in the story of the storm on the Galilean lake which Jesus stilled (if he did) the question was asked by his disciples in the boat on the now calm water, 'Who then is this that even the wind and sea obey him?' (Mark 4.41). This is the right question to ask in the presence of the miracles of Jesus: *what do they tell us about HIM?* Of what are they the sign? One fact stands out: far from being stunts, everyone of them was carried out to help people in need, whether illness, crippling or bereavement – and this was true of the nature miracles. Always Jesus was caring for and about people and his miracles are signs that God is like that, God is not the absentee Lord of his creation, he stands by always ready to help. No, do not rub out the miracles of Jesus lest you rub out what you and I most need, the assurance that God cares.

There is more to be said on this subject but I shall have to leave it over till another sermon.

8

GOD AND MAN

God was in Christ reconciling the world to himself.

2 CORINTHIANS 5.19

A few Sunday evenings ago I watched the BBC programme called *Songs of Praise*. I make a point of doing this from time to time, not least because it is a way of keeping in touch with other forms of Christian worship than that to which I am normally accustomed, and in passing let me comment on how well these programmes are presented. This particular programme was broadcast not from some parish church in the heart of the country but from a Methodist church in central London. The singing was led not by organ and choir but by a band powerful and vigorous, enlivened with modern rhythms. The place was packed with young people who obviously revelled in the hymns. It was a simple faith they expressed centred on Jesus and what he had done for them. Then at the close of the service a minister pronounced the blessing 'God the Father, God the Son, God the Holy Spirit be with you always'. It sounded so complicated after the simplicity of the hymns, and so puzzling if anyone stopped to think. Why is not a straightforward devotion to Jesus enough? We can read about the historical Jesus, some would say, 'the real Jesus, the man of Galilee' and try to follow him, why does the Church drag in this Trinitarian formula which few people understand? This however is what the Prayer Book (ASB) says we believe. 'We believe in one Lord Jesus Christ, the only Son of God, eternally begotten of the Father, God from God, Light from Light, true God from true God, begotten not made, of one Being with the Father.' It all seems a long way from Jesus of Nazareth. What are we to make of it? It puzzles people.

1 HOW WAS JESUS GOD?

In the last sermon I spoke about the difficulties some people have with the miracles of Jesus on the grounds that they conflict with the modern scientific understanding of the universe. I should not be surprised however if some others didn't say to themselves 'But this doesn't worry me at all. After all don't we believe that Jesus was God? Surely nothing is beyond the power of God. Jesus worked the miracles of which we read in the gospels because he was God.' Yes, but we also read that Jesus on occasion was tired, that he was hungry and that he asked for information. Was this play-acting? Or was he really a man with the limitations that manhood involves? The answer is that he was both God and man. But how could he be both? This is the problem of Jesus and why, gratified as we may be that he has become much more real to us through modern presentations of the historical Jesus, we cannot stop there, we still have to ask who he was, and there certainly can be no Christian faith until we wrestle with the problem till we have an answer.

Let me begin by looking at some *unsatisfactory answers*. Jesus was not God in the full sense nor was he man in the full sense. He was something in between, so neither really God nor really man. He was a mythical kind of being, a concept quite familiar in pagan religion. This is not what we believe, this is not what we preach. Nor do we believe that Jesus was inhabiting a human body for thirty years or so, so that the physical body was human but his mind or spirit was divine, which means that in Jesus God took on a temporary disguise. Nor do we believe that Jesus began by being a man but grew into divinity, indeed the word 'divinity' is never used for him in the New Testament. He was God, he is God, he did not become divine. Nor do we believe that God for a period of thirty years or so changed into a man. God does not change. This then is not what the Incarnation means. From all this it will be seen that the problem is centred on the Incarnation. There certainly are difficulties how to interpret it. One of the most recent attempts to find a solution is to cut the historical cord altogether. The Incarnation is to be understood metaphorically not literally: Jesus lived in such close communion with God that in his person he incarnated God as it were, which means that the belief in the pre-existence of Jesus as the *Logos* has to be dropped in spite of its place in the New Testament and in the faith held by the Church.

2 PARADOX

So there are no easy answers. But there is an answer, though not an easy one and I cannot claim to have found it by myself but have learnt it from a teacher more learned, wiser and more deeply committed to the Christian faith than I could ever be. The answer is, we have to understand Jesus as *God and man* as a paradox, the dictionary definition of which is 'an assertion seemingly absurd but really correct'. What is more, paradox is deeply embedded in the Christian experience. The good which the Christian possesses is something of which he does not boast as if it were wholly due to his own achievement. He says in the words of St Paul 'by the grace of God I am what I am' or, in the words of the familiar hymn, 'And every virtue we possess, And every victory won, And every thought of holiness, Are his alone.' This attitude of attributing all to God does not however do away with personal responsibility. Both are responsible for the good in the Christian's life, God's grace and human effort, both together are the cause. So there is paradox at the very heart of the Christian experience. Ought we therefore to be surprised to find paradox in the person of Jesus himself? He is God and man. This is what we believe. This is what we preach.

I come back again for a moment to those miracles which Jesus is said in the gospels to have wrought. We are not to see here God using the man Jesus as a kind of passive instrument so as to enable us to assert that God was working them, no wonder they took place. No, these were the works of the man Jesus who lived so wholly in communion with God that there was available to him God's power to achieve them. Jesus was there and God was there – the paradox. And this applies not only to the wonderful works but also to the wonderful words of Jesus which is why we do not read them as merely the outcropping of human wisdom. Not that Jesus wrote them. He never wrote anything except once in the sand, so easy to be rubbed out with the foot, and they may not have been words he wrote (see John 8.6). What we have in the gospels is the evangelists' reporting and interpretation of what he said. But through them we can hear God speaking to us. Through the operation of the Holy Spirit they become to us the word of God.

3 THE PRE-EXISTENCE AND ETERNITY OF JESUS

Now because we believe that Jesus is God and man we cannot think that Jesus came into existence at the Incarnation. God has existed from all eternity and God will exist for all eternity to come. He is the eternal God. This is true also of Jesus. And so we speak of the pre-existence of Jesus and of his continued ministry in every age. The Nicene Creed expresses this in concrete terms: 'Who for us men, and for our salvation came down from heaven'. And then: 'And ascended into heaven, And sitteth on the right hand of the Father.' Picture language certainly, but what else can be employed? Difficult to grasp of course but this at least is obvious: we have moved a long way from counting the story of the historical Jesus as sufficient for us, gripping as it undoubtedly is and never to be left behind, it is fundamental. We are led however to ask about God as he is in himself. To put the matter in a nutshell. Because of the Incarnation we now speak of God as a Trinity. 'God in three persons, blessed Trinity.'

But how then are we to understand the 'three persons'? God the Father, God the Son, God the Holy Spirit. Does this mean that God shows himself in three modes of being, sometimes as Father, sometimes as Son, sometimes as Holy Spirit? The Church thinks not. Or does it envisage three distinct personal

Gods? Again the Church thinks not. Perhaps the subject is beyond useful discussion. How can we ever grasp what is the nature of God in himself? But we for our part do *experience* the One God in three different ways as Father, Son and Holy Spirit and maybe we shall be wise to leave the matter there, especially in a sermon!

*　　*　　*

And now in closing let me appeal to you. Do not grow impatient with these creeds and their complicated formulas about Jesus. They were drawn up to protect our faith in Jesus of Nazareth, not in some prearranged academic situation, they were hammered out in conflict, some of it I regret to say most unattractive, even with fisticuffs involved. A few minutes ago I listed some of the wrong answers to the question how Jesus could be both God and man. I could have attached names to these propositions and told how some of them almost overtook what the Church was to believe and preach. But they came to be labelled 'heresies'; by the year AD 451 however at the Council of Chalcedon what the Church believed about Jesus was established and accepted and still is accepted as the Catholic faith. The complaint has often been made against it that it consists largely of negatives, it tells us what we are not to believe about how Jesus is God and man. There is truth in this, but the point for us to grasp is that it acts as a kind of protective fence around our faith in Jesus, and fences are not generally attractive, but they are necessary. So I appeal to you. Love the story of Jesus of Nazareth. Learn all you can about him. You will never exhaust all that it has to say. But do not make the mistake of thinking, this is enough for me, I need no more. You need to understand who Jesus is. He did not come merely to show us what God is like – no, *he is God* once incarnate among us, God and man, from all eternity past and eternity to come, or as the *Te Deum* expresses it, 'Thou art the King of glory: O Christ. Thou art the everlasting Son of the Father.'

9
ETERNAL LIFE

I am the resurrection and the life; he who believes in me, though he die, yet shall he live, and whoever lives and believes in me shall never die.

JOHN 11.25, 26 (RSV)

This is Easter Day, the Sunday the Christian Church sets higher than any other, indeed all our Sundays exist because of it. Not surprisingly therefore we have bigger congregations today, the worship is buoyant and we spend time and money decorating our churches with flowers. This is a joyous day, a day for uplifted hearts and, dare I hope, shining faces too.

Jesus Christ is risen today – Alleluia.

But many people will stay away. The church bells will ring out loud and clear but a high percentage of the public will not be stirred. They would miss the bells of course if this was a silent Easter Day as in the war years 1939–45, and enquire the reason. But why are they absent? Is it because faith has generally slipped out? People do not believe as once they did. They do not hear any message, any gospel, any good news. Christian faith has slipped out. Why then do some of us persist in believing in Easter?

1 THE TRADITION OF BELIEF

First, because we have been brought up to it. I know this sounds tame but it is true. We would like it to be said that we have all sifted the evidence for the resurrection of Christ on Easter Day and have come to the conclusion that it holds together. It happened. I believe it did but most of us are not students. We accept Easter because we were brought up in the tradition of belief. And tradition is not to be despised. It shapes the way we live, how we think, what we believe. There has for long been a lively debate, especially in America, on how Christians become Christians in the first place. Is it by evangelism or is it by nurture? Both have their part to play but it cannot be denied that evangelism is most effective where there has already been a degree of Christian nurture, and evangelism for its part only has lasting results if it is followed up by such nurture. Never therefore underrate the power and importance of tradition. Do not dismiss your belief in Easter, my belief, or anyone else's belief simply because we were nurtured in it. The faith of the community to which we belong counts and it is a serious matter to break with it, for the breaking leaves people adrift.

I go further. Do everything to strengthen the traditional belief. See that the children receive an Easter egg or some other present. Let the day be marked as a holiday, maybe with an outing for good measure. Yes, these are superfluities but it is by such simple devices that Easter gains its first entry into the lives of ordinary people forming a gateway for belief, even later, it is to be hoped, of informed belief. I am not ashamed to confess that I, the preacher, began to believe in Easter because when I was a small boy my mother saw to it that I was excited by the discovery of an Easter egg on the breakfast table. I liked Easter.

But now Easter has taken a beating. In recent years questions have been asked, doubts have been raised and desertions have taken place from the traditional faith. Our churches are not as full as they were. This however is the striking fact. Easter has never been wiped out; whatever the assaults it has sustained, it keeps coming back. At times it appears like a ship at sea apparently certain to be overcome by the waves and the fierceness of the criticisms which engulf it, but it survives, weatherbeaten, and it rides out the storms not merely afloat but the bearer still of people and goods to the chosen destination. This is part of the marvel of Easter, its astonishing survival capability. No wonder many of us believe it, no wonder it is still preached.

2 THE MEANING OF EASTER

But what does Easter mean? What does it mean for us in our world of computers, space travel and telecommunications? Even if we are convinced that the resurrection of Jesus happened, what relevance can an event two thousand years ago have for contemporary man and woman? Just this: we all have to die but death is not a final event, this is what Easter has to say to us. But it looks as if it is, we cannot deny it. And if the resurrection of Jesus did not take place, and the stories in the New Testament about it are pure fabrication, then no one has ever come back from the grave and we can be certain no one ever will. Death really is the dead end. But Easter happened and this is what it has to say: there is a future *beyond death*, and the festival called the Ascension has something specific to say about it. (I will preach on this on another occasion.)

For the present however we cannot escape death. It is an indisputable fact of our mortality. And so death is wreathed around with the pain of sadness sometimes almost unbearable, and funerals are bound to be mournful. Anyone who has really loved and lost will know of the darkness that descends upon the human spirit when at the crematorium those curtains slowly close and the precious body is gone for ever. What a mercy if then we can remember Jesus, what he said, what he did and what the Church came to believe about him and what it preaches in the light of Easter.

And now let me remind you of one of the most illuminating stories on all this as recorded in St John's gospel, chapter 11. It is about the death of a man called Lazarus whom Jesus loved along with his sisters Martha and Mary. So the context of the incident is a close bond of human affection which Jesus shared with these three people. But death stepped in, leaving two heart-broken sisters; and Lazarus was in his grave before Jesus returned from a journey. When he came there and saw the mourners consoling Martha and when he saw Mary crying he broke down himself. People saw the tears streaming down his face. Where there is love there are bound to be tears in the presence of death. Jesus showed himself to be human no more clearly than when he stood there by Lazarus' grave crying. Never can we suggest that in the case of a Christian burial there should be no mourning. Jesus wept. But Jesus had already said to Martha 'I am the resurrection and the life; he who believes in me, though he die, yet shall he live, and whoever lives and believes in me shall never die'.

What did he mean, and what can these words say to us? Manifestly they cannot refer to physical death. Lazarus, a believer, was already in his grave when Jesus uttered them. Clearly the man or woman who believes in Jesus dies just like any other man or woman. Death holds back from no one. So when Jesus said 'whoever lives and believes in me shall never die' he was not promising escape from death. He was saying that our relationship with Jesus cannot be broken by death. And the life anyone has by that faith is *God's life in him* and so it can never come to an end, for God cannot die. Physical death therefore is powerless to destroy this kind of life. Thus the belief in life after death is grounded in a new basis, not in the nature of the soul, not in the nature of man, indeed not in anything human but in a relationship with Jesus Christ and through him with God. We have become indissolubly linked with him who conquered death at Easter and so life cannot be ended by death.

3 LIFE NOW

Have I spent rather a long time on this aspect of Easter in my sermon? But I am not morbid, I am a realist. Of course we long for the joy of Easter, the triumphant singing and the Church decorated with flowers, but that joy will not be lasting and survive the dark days if we will persist in sidestepping the fact of death which sooner or later will face us all, and, more hurting still perhaps, the death of those who are 'all the world to us'. Forgive me if I am wrong but it seems to me that even the

Church is guilty of avoiding this subject, leaving the bereaved so without an anchor that they come asking for a special service to help them in the days they are experiencing as hopelessly dark. What is required is more preaching than there is about what we believe concerning life after death, and the wisdom to preach it.

And now let me touch on other aspects of the Easter gospel than the one I have stressed in this sermon. Jesus is the resurrection and the life, he said so. The reference is not only to life after death but the life now in this life, what is called in the New Testament eternal life, not, I hasten to add, life which goes on for ever and ever, which could be anything but a blessing, indeed in some circumstances more like a curse. No, it means the opposite of spiritual death, in the wake of which there so quickly follows moral death and even intellectual death. Sometimes, I fear, we are coming close to these kinds of death in the life of our community today. The reason is we have retreated from belief in Jesus Christ. Perhaps we have not heard, or not understood, or consciously written off the words of Jesus, 'he that believeth in me shall never die', that is, in this life as we go about our manifold duties and pleasures. Sadly it is possible to be dead to all that is fine, noble, uplifting and buoyant and to sink down into a moral and spiritual lethargy, a kind of living death. When shall we learn that to believe in the God made known to us in Christ is *the way to be alive?* This is the Easter message, this is the Easter Gospel. 'I am the resurrection and the life, saith the Lord, he that believeth in me, though he were dead, yet shall he live: and he that believeth in me shall never die.'

'Shall never die'. What a promise! Not to be dead as you go about your work tomorrow, catching the same train, struggling to endure seemingly interminable traffic jams, wading through that pile of papers on the desk and waiting yet again in that shopping queue. Not to be dead in the home circle, not to be dead to whatever appeals that come for help for the world's needy and not only in Bosnia but nearer home. Easter offers us life now, in the winter as well as in the spring. Can we believe it? Can we preach it? Life through uniting ourselves with the living God by faith: Jesus Christ the Lord. Then let the bells ring out! Let the anthems be raised. Eternal life now, this is the message of Easter. Alleluia!

10
HEAVEN

We are sown a natural body but we are raised a spiritual body.

1 CORINTHIANS 15.44 (RSV)

If there is one Collect from the Book of Common Prayer I shall never forget, and can even repeat in my sleep, it is that appointed for the Sixth Sunday after Trinity. 'O God, who hast prepared for them that love thee such good things as pass man's understanding: Pour into our hearts such love toward thee, that we, loving thee above all things, may obtain thy promises, which exceed all that we can desire; through Jesus Christ our Lord.' I will tell you why. From the ages of fourteen to eighteen I heard it from the pulpit of the church I attended with my family as the preface to every sermon, yes, every sermon, almost without exception whatever the Sunday, whatever the occasion. I am unlikely to forget it.

1 THE QUESTION OF AGEING

This constant reference to heaven would sound odd in today's world, even in today's Church. The clergy on the whole have gone quiet about the subject. All the concentration today is on making the best of life in this world and helping others to make the best of it too. Welfare is in the air, it is the key word, for many the very essence of religion. One of the reasons for this is the vast improvement in the quality of life, due largely to human effort, with the result that there is a heightened expectation of what can be obtained from life. This has caused a decline of interest in a life beyond this life. The aim is to make the most of the here and now, anything else is doubtful and problematical. Heaven is not therefore seriously considered.

But we do grow older, all of us, and with it the unavoidable experience of ageing. This is something we are not allowed to forget these days. And since people live longer than was the case even ten years ago, ageing is a growing problem in the community. There are more old people to be cared for now, and more welfare necessary, more carers, and more income support of one kind and another, and with all this a growing concern how the diminishing working population can support all this financially. At the same time the age for retirement is now reckoned to be 60, even lower, and so there is a large section of the population needing guidance how to occupy themselves in these ageing years. Retirement is a frightening prospect. For this reason there is a growing number of organizations brought into existence to help with what is often called *the problem of retirement*. The advice to the ageing, and it is good advice, is not simply to sit back, though it is wise to ease up. Older people have skills which can be employed on a voluntary basis for the benefit of the community and for the individual concerned. Keeping active in body and mind contributes to health both physically and mentally.

All this is true and should be taken seriously. What is sometimes called the 'rocking chair' existence is not to be recommended for the ageing. The stubborn fact however remains: life does close in as we grow older. I remember the late Lord Fisher, one time Archbishop of Canterbury, a most vigorous and energetic man, saying not long after he retired from Lambeth Palace and Sherborne: 'I only rarely go to London now, it is too tiring!' And so his life was narrowing to his village, then to his house and garden, then to one room, and finally to his bed. His life in fact narrowed with age. It does. But I also remember him saying this: 'I look forward to passing over to the other side. I have so many questions I have never been able to solve in my life and I look forward to having the answers.' Was he thinking of the text from that famous chapter 13 of St Paul's first letter to the Corinthians? 'For now we see in a mirror dimly, but then face to face. Now I know in part; then I shall understand fully, even as I have been fully understood.' Not for him therefore was the ageing process a slow and rather miserable grind down to who knows what, but a buoyant pilgrimage up to a glorious future of thrilling realization of what had only been half experienced, in other words heaven; or as the Collect for the Sixth Sunday after Trinity has it: 'O God, who has prepared for them that love thee such good things as pass man's understanding . . .', that is, heaven.

2 TWO OPPOSING VIEWS OF IMMORTALITY

Now what is involved here is a firm belief in life after death. Not everyone shares this belief. Not long ago a man who was doing a job for me in my garden said to me out of the blue 'You know there is a difference between you and me. I believe that when we die we are done for, there is nothing else.' I have wondered since if he was 'flying a kite' to see what I would say, if he was not confessing his real conviction. In any case, in a sentence or two I said what I believed. But why do some of us, a great many of us, believe in life after death? In what way do we understand it? There are two views on this which I will briefly explain.

First there is the doctrine of the immortality of souls. I do not myself assent to this but it has a long history, being current among the ancient Greeks. I will put it first. As an individual the human being consists of two parts, the material and the immaterial, that is the body and the soul. At death this essential unity is sundered. The body, the natural part, is destined for dissolution in the grave or its equivalent, in other words it perishes, in the comment of my odd-job man it is 'done for'. The immaterial part however, the soul, has within it the seed of immortality, it does not die with the dissolution of the body, on the contrary, freed from the prison of the flesh, it flies up like a liberated bird to live in paradise as a disembodied spirit. Heaven then consists of the company of such immortal souls or disembodied spirits.

Over against this is the doctrine of the resurrection of the body, often dismissed as crude and unintelligent in comparison with the doctrine of the immortality of the soul, but it is the biblical view. It does not count the physical body of the individual of little intrinsic worth and therefore without a future. It sees the human body and the human spirit as *together* making one comprehensive whole, each part influencing the other and making for the individuality of the person. At death the body decays but is not lost, it is raised to newness of life and in this resurrection body the spirit of the individual lives. Heaven then is peopled not with disembodied spirits but with recognizable persons, different from but not discontinuous with the persons known in the here and now. This is the doctrine of the resurrection of the body. We confess our belief in this in the Apostles' Creed, recited regularly in the course of public worship: 'I believe in the Resurrection of the body, And the life everlasting'. This does not mean resurrection of the flesh: 'body' here means person, personality, individuality. St Paul was quite dogmatic on this. He wrote to the Corinthians 'flesh and blood cannot inherit the kingdom of God, nor does the perishable inherit the imperishable' (1 Cor 15.50 RSV). He believed that 'we are sown a natural body but we are raised a spiritual body', a belief which spurred him on to the triumphal climax in this argument: 'For the trumpet shall sound, and the dead shall be raised imperishable, and we shall be changed. For this perishable nature must put on the imperishable, and this mortal nature must put on immortality. When the perishable puts on the imperishable, and the mortal puts on immortality, then shall be brought to pass the saying that is written: "Death is swallowed up in victory" ' (1 Cor 15.52–54 RSV). There is of course much that we do not know of this future and we must be restrained in our comment, but that does not mean uncertainty. We read the confident words in 1 John 3.2 (RSV): 'it does not yet appear what we shall be, but we know that when he appears we shall be like him, for we shall see him as he is.'

What then is the essential difference between these two views of the life after death? It can be put in a nutshell. The doctrine of the immortality of the soul grounds it in what each person intrinsically possesses. The doctrine of the resurrection of the body, on the other hand, looks to the resurrection of Christ on Easter Day and our immortality not as ours by nature but as God's gift to us through Christ. 1 Timothy 6.16 is quite categorical, God 'alone has immortality'. We do not possess it in our own right.

3 REVERENT AGNOSTICISM

And now let me leave off being a theological teacher in the pulpit and speak in my true role as a pastoral preacher. I have had my fair share of ministering to people beaten down by bereavement and I have been through it myself, an experience which can only really be known from the inside. People ask me, shall we recognize each other in the afterlife? I guess the question is prompted by the first view I enunciated, the doctrine of the immortality of the soul. How can disembodied spirits know each other again in the afterlife? It is a reasonable question, for are we not known through our bodies? What attraction can there be in a community of disembodied spirits? On the second view I propounded we shall be different in heaven but recognizably you and recognizably me. Will then the man be met as a man and the woman as a woman? Or are the dwellers in heaven sexless beings? Earlier this year my eye was caught by an article in a very respectable monthly theological journal called *The Expository Times*. It was headed 'Sex in heaven'. I started. What? Surely sex isn't being dragged into heaven! What next? I would not have taken offence if the title had read 'Gender in heaven?' for it was simply introducing the question I have just raised. Will the gender difference between men and women exist in heaven? The writer of the article thought so, for individuality cannot be separated from gender, and went on to point to the dispute Jesus had with the Sadducees when they tried to catch him with a 'cock and bull story' about a woman who had had seven husbands one after another who all died. In the resurrection, the Sadducees mockingly asked, 'Whose wife will she be of the seven?' Jesus' reply was not that there is no such thing as differentiation of gender in heaven; he said there is no such thing as marriage. Now what shall I, the preacher, say about this? There are many hard questions that can be asked about the life after death, for example, 'will children who die in infancy always be children?' On this kind of question we shall be wise to remain agnostic, but reverent agnostic. For myself I am content to rest with 1 John 3.2: 'Beloved, we are God's children now; it does not yet appear what we shall be, but we know that when he appears we shall be like him, for we shall see him as he is.'

So I bid you, do not be frightened of heaven. It will be all right. More than that, far more, it will be a place of wonder, happiness and contentment, yes and activity, or in words far better than I could ever frame:

> O God, who hast prepared for them that love thee such good things as pass man's understanding: Pour into our hearts such love toward thee, that we, loving thee above all things, may obtain thy promises, which exceed all that we can desire; through Jesus Christ our Lord. Amen. (Collect for the Sixth Sunday after Trinity, BCP)

11

THIS SAME JESUS

'. . . this same Jesus, which is taken up from you into heaven, shall so come in like manner as ye have seen him go into heaven.

ACTS 1.11 (AV)

Dorothy L. Sayers (1893–1957), the playwright, is best known perhaps as the creator of Lord Peter Wimsey, but she was also no mean theologian. In a small book she presented the life of the historical Jesus as 'the greatest drama ever staged'. The drama was played out not in some theatre but among the people of Galilee and Judaea when Pilate was governor of Judaea during the Roman occupation.

Now every drama must have an ending, of course it must, there has to be a final curtain, but in the case of 'the greatest drama ever staged' when was it? Was it the crucifixion? Was the last that was seen of Jesus of Nazareth his removal as a corpse from that horrible cross at Golgotha outside Jerusalem's city walls? No doubt it seemed to be. The enormity of it would never be forgotten. But had the curtain really come down? Were there not people ready to testify to his resurrection from the grave? They had seen the risen Christ. Nevertheless the curtain had to come down even on these resurrection appearances. But when and how? The event is described in Acts, chapter 1, verse 9 and is called 'the Ascension'. It reads: 'When he had said this, as they watched, he was lifted up and a cloud removed him from their sight.'

1 THE PROBLEM OF HISTORICITY

We boggle at this. Of course we do. It reflects a completely outmoded astronomy, a flat earth with heaven up above the blue sky, the Ptolemaic view of the world. How can the Church celebrate this event, because it certainly has celebrated it? The primitive Church constantly and consistently preached it. But why? We do not normally celebrate someone's departure unless we hate him. The Ascension however stands as one of the great festivals of the Christian year along with Christmas, Easter and Pentecost. Clearly this fact forces us to turn our attention to *the significance* of the event and by what means we can come to terms with the historical aspect. For myself I am prepared to say that something (but exactly what?) so unusual and so striking took place as to impress on the minds of the disciples of Jesus that they were seeing him for the last time, the curtain was coming down on the greatest drama ever staged, God manifest on earth as a man, a real human being.

All this being so, we must rest our attention, not on what precisely happened at the Ascension, for this we can never know, but what it signifies, what it means, indeed what it means for us. This I believe is summed up in the word 'exaltation' or 'elevation' and the passage of Scripture which points most clearly to this is in St Paul's letter to the Church at Philippi, chapter 2, verses 7–11: 'Bearing the human likeness, revealed in human shape, he humbled himself, and in obedience accepted even death – death on a cross. Therefore God raised him to the heights and bestowed on him the name above all names, that at the name of Jesus every knee should bow – in heaven, on earth, and in the depths – and every tongue confess, "Jesus Christ is Lord", to the glory of God the Father.' We are not unfamiliar in ordinary life with elevation of this kind, elevation to a peerage, to a managerial position, even a statue lifted high in the capital. We say they have 'gone up in the world', they have ascended. Poor as no doubt these examples are as illustrations of the Ascension which the Church celebrates, they at least point to the way of conceiving it, we may even say believing it, leaving aside when and where and how exactly it took place as Acts, chapter 1 describes it, for we can never know.

2 THE MEANING OF THE ASCENSION

And now the meaning of the Ascension, the meaning for us. We know now that the curtain has *not* come down on the historical Jesus and never will come down. Jesus is not simply a figure in the past. I have reverted to the Authorized Version for the text of this sermon because I want to highlight the way it stresses the continuity of Jesus *as Jesus* for ever even though he has been exalted to the highest. 'This same Jesus' the text says. It is a legitimate way to translate the three Greek words which open it though I concede 'This Jesus' would do. 'This same Jesus' however *drives home* the point that the Jesus whom the disciples encountered in Galilee and Judaea, talked with, laughed with, shared meals with, slept rough out in the open sometimes with, faced storm and tempest with, and the cruel words and onslaught of those who hated all he stood for, *this same Jesus* is he who is now King, King of Heaven, King of the universe, King of that sphere beyond the grave to which we all one day will come. I must speak for myself – please forgive me – I find this most comforting. When I reflect how patient was Jesus with the sheer woodenness of the disciples on more occasions than one, how ready he was to forgive their faults, how accepting of their various differences, but each one valued for his own sake, and *this same Jesus* is King of heaven, I breathe a huge sigh of relief, then there is room for the likes of me; if this is what the Ascension means, *means for me*, I want to celebrate it. And when my time comes and I pass through the gate of death my fear of what lies on the other side is taken away. *This same Jesus* will be there; exactly how I do not know but *this same Jesus* will have a place for me and for those I love.

There has risen up in the last few years a kind of antipathy to what is called 'Jesus religion'. I understand this. It can be cheap and sentimental, too weak to produce strength of mind and purpose in those who are caught by it. It glosses over difficulties. It does not face problems. If however this opposition causes us to underrate *the eternal significance* of the historical Jesus, the man Jesus, we shall be wise to resist it. We must learn all we can about him who walked about in Galilee and Judaea, and hold him at the centre of our Christian faith and practice. He, it is, who gives us confidence to face the future whatever comes, he knows us and understands us, all our struggles and all our weakness, we are safe with 'this same Jesus'.

3 OUR HUMANITY DIGNIFIED

And now something else: the Ascension dignifies our common humanity. The Incarnation of course does this. That the Godhead could be disclosed through the medium of a human life is remarkable. It says volumes about the intrinsic worth of our human nature that it should be counted capable of being the medium for such a disclosure, for despair about human nature almost plagues us in the modern world. Yes, science and technology have improved the quality of life on a widespread, if not worldwide, scale but suicidal wars proliferate and, as a result, cruelty, famine, hunger and disease. Human skills are refined but then sharpened into yet more sophisticated weapons of destruction. Perhaps we could understand if God rated human nature as fit only for the scrap heap. And then we remember that he made us and is not far from any one of us, indeed 'in him we live and move and have our being' whether we are aware of the fact or not. Human nature is not 'written off'. The Incarnation, God revealed in a human life, the life of Jesus, tells the opposite; and when *this same Jesus* is raised to the throne of heaven we can be certain that this is so.

Every now and again there arises some man, some woman, who by their caring ministry demonstrates the worth of every human person whatever the apparent indications to the contrary. Mother Teresa cared for the wrecks of human beings abandoned on the streets of Calcutta like rubbish simply because they were human, not because they might possibly be of some use in the world. Mother Teresa, and others like her, see humanity as God sees it, something of infinite worth. This is the message of the Ascension. It was the human Jesus that was beaten to death who was elevated to the heights, not simply his spirit but the man, 'this same Jesus'. People are not rubbish, however battered. To respect this when the time comes they must be given a decent burial.

4 JUBILATION BECAUSE JESUS IS EXALTED

We believe in the Ascension of Jesus. How could we not believe it? His elevation in the world is obvious. Is there anyone more well-known than Jesus, any name more on the lips of men and women across the whole world than that of Jesus? Clearly he *is* exalted, he *is* raised on high, he is no more the local man of Nazareth. He is on the throne, the One by which all that is best, highest and noblest is measured. Yes, we believe in the Ascension. The Church celebrates it and proclaims it. The gospel is enshrined in it.

The appropriate response to the Ascension is jubilation. Churches should pick up their Psalters and find Psalm 47 for Ascensiontide. Then if they are fortunate enough to possess a competent choir they should drum up all the members and add on any singers they can muster; more than that, bring out whatever musical instruments and players may be available in addition to the organ, and then . . . Psalm 47, verse 6 put into operation. 'O sing praises, sing praises unto our God, O sing praises; sing praises unto our King.' And a clatter of cymbals and tambourines wouldn't be out of place, nor hand-clapping and maybe dancing. And if the neighbourhood wonders what is going on in that local church with all its jubilation and they are told that the Ascension of Christ is being celebrated, what a loud proclamation of the gospel this would be. 'O clap your hands together, all ye people . . . For the Lord is high . . . he is the great King upon all the earth.' This is what we believe, this is what we preach, this is what we celebrate.

12
GOD THE HOLY SPIRIT

When the day of Pentecost had come, they were all together in one place. And suddenly a sound came from heaven like the rush of a mighty wind, . . . And they were all filled with the Holy Spirit.

ACTS 2.1, 2, 4 (RSV)

I have my work 'cut out' in this sermon, and so have you, because the subject is the Holy Spirit and it isn't easy to grasp. God the Creator, this we can appreciate, for we see the creation around us and wonder at it, indeed never cease to wonder. Jesus Christ we can appreciate, he walked about in Judaea and Galilee as a man, people actually laid hold of him, astonishing thought! But the Holy Spirit, ah! this is different, you can't lay hold of a spirit. No wonder we are somewhat mystified. Perhaps the compilers of the Apostles' Creed were puzzled too, for they present us with a clear statement of God the Creator, calling him the maker of heaven and earth; and then follow with quite a summary of the life and death of Jesus 'his only Son our Lord'; but when stage three is reached, only this: 'I believe in the Holy Ghost', full stop. Didn't they know what to say? The fuller Nicene Creed of course, which we recite in the Service of Holy Communion, expands this bald statement. 'I believe in the Holy Ghost, The Lord and giver of life, Who proceedeth from the Father and the Son. Who with the Father and the Son together is worshipped and glorified, Who spake by the Prophets.' And if we are forced to admit that this amplification does not really tell us what the Holy Spirit *is*, it certainly tells us what he *does*, what is his function: he is the giver of life. This is the point at which we could begin to grasp our difficult subject.

1 A MIGHTY WIND

Let us then begin with the simple statement that the concept of the Holy Spirit tells us how God is present and active in the world now. He works in the world as his Spirit, creating new situations and opportunities, bringing life and making for community. This makes our subject contemporary and if we do dwell on an historical event, that is, the day of Pentecost when the disciples of the risen Christ were all together in one place and there came from heaven a sound like the rush of a mighty wind, it is to mark the point at which the activity of God as the Holy Spirit was strikingly seen and felt. If then we confess that we believe in the Holy Spirit, what we are doing is confessing that *God is at work in the world* now, in events and in the lives of men and women today. This makes for a dynamic understanding of Christianity. No place, no man or woman, or community where the Holy Spirit is present is ever dead; the Spirit is 'the Lord and Giver of life'. The Holy Spirit indicates action, energetic action.

The picture word which conjures up the concept of the Spirit is wind. No, not a gentle breeze which we enjoy for its refreshment in the garden, or on the seafront, but a tearing, rushing mighty wind. The Hebrews had a distinctive word for it – *ruach*. It was different from the Greek word *pneuma* which we have in our words 'pneumatic' and 'pneumonia', referring to air or breath. *Ruach* spoke of energy, it accomplished spectacular results. Nothing was ever quite the same after *ruach* had blown over it. I can never think of this without remembering that night in October 1987 when the wind altered my garden and it has never been the same since. I had a small orchard but when the light broke in the morning, there was no orchard; almost every tree had been ripped out of the ground and the garden fences were down. It took nearly a year to clear the place, replan and replant it. This is what the wind did in one night. It was *ruach* all right, a rushing, mighty wind. It illuminated for me how the writer of the Acts of the Apostles understood the activity of God as Spirit energizing the apostles gathered together. He wrote 'When the day of Pentecost had come they were all together in one place. And suddenly a sound came from heaven like the rush of a mighty wind . . . And they were all filled with the Holy Spirit.' This thought must have gone back to Genesis, chapter 1, verses 1 and 2 – and I am going to quote from the New English Bible: 'In the beginning of Creation, when God made heaven and earth, the earth was without form and void, with darkness over the face of the abyss, and a mighty wind [the word is *ruach*] that swept over the surface of the waters.' The Revised Standard Version follows the usual translation and reads '*the Spirit of God* was moving over the face of the waters' but there is a footnote 'or wind'. We can therefore hardly avoid the conclusion: the picture word for the Holy Spirit in the Bible is a strong and mighty wind. This is how we are to understand the Holy Spirit. It is God's energetic, transforming activity in the world. The Holy Spirit is God *at work*, creating, making, remaking, breaking down barriers and opening up new prospects. Pentecost was the day when this was plain to see.

2 EXTRAORDINARY GROWTH

And so St Luke, the author of the Acts of the Apostles, told the story of the extraordinary growth of the Christian Church from its initiation in Jerusalem on the day of Pentecost. The nucleus was a dozen men who had lived in the company of Jesus throughout the whole of his ministry and were also witnesses of his resurrection. Quickly that nucleus broke out of the limitations of its beginning. It was thrusting, bold and effective. It was not a movement to be ignored. It set people talking, arguing and attacking. Very soon it was operative in Samaria which no good Jew would touch and then way up north in Antioch, then across the sea to Cyprus, then to what is now Asia Minor, after that the great venture over the water to Europe, as we now know it, and to crown all, to Rome itself; all that within thirty years, and Churches founded in all these places. This was God at work as his Holy Spirit, like a strong mighty wind able to be battled against but not stopped. And today there are Churches around the globe and the Christians are numbered in millions. This story is not told, or should not be told, with triumphalism as its motivation. This is not a human success story, far from it. What it shows is the way in which God is experienced since Jesus no longer walked the earth. He is known in the energetic activity of his Holy Spirit like a strong and mighty wind, *ruach*, God's creative power.

3 FELLOWSHIP AND COMMUNITY

I come back now to the Nicene Creed. The word 'believe' occurs four times, that is at the opening of each of the four paragraphs. 'We believe in one God . . . We believe in one Lord, Jesus Christ . . . We believe in the Holy Spirit' and then this: 'We believe in one holy catholic and apostolic Church' (I am following the wording of the Alternative Service Book). The point I ask you to notice is how the thought of the Holy Spirit passes at once to the Church. Of course it does, the Church was founded on the day when the Holy Spirit made the fellowship and common life of the Church possible. We read in the book of the Acts of the Apostles, chapter 2, how the apostles were 'all together in one place', the togetherness in Jerusalem being at the express command of the risen Christ, but they were twelve individuals together, their individualism prominent and rightly so. They were united of course in following Jesus and above all in being witnesses of his resurrection, but they were only bound together in a fellowship with a common life *when the Holy Spirit came upon them*. This then was the birthday of the Christian Church.

It would be easy for us to respond to this piece of Christian history with the words 'Oh how interesting', but it has something important to say to the Church now. All too easily we assume that the Church can be organized into existence, but the secret of its life is not in organization. Organization has its part to play, and incompetent organization can be disastrous, especially where money is involved, but without the dynamism of the Spirit the Church is a dead machine, its wheels turning over, but not productive of life. The Spirit comes upon a community when it believes with its whole heart the gospel of the death and resurrection of Jesus, and responds to the preaching of it. This is brought out nowhere more clearly than in the tenth chapter of the book of the Acts of the Apostles, which may appropriately be called the account of the second Pentecost. Those on whom the Spirit descended were not Jews, they were not apostles, the event did not take place in the holy city of Jerusalem but in the Roman garrison town of Caesarea down on the Mediterranean coast. A congregation had been assembled by a centurion, a Roman army major. He had gathered together a diverse group of friends and relatives, everyone a Gentile, that is, a non-Jew, and the purpose was to hear St Peter preach the Christian gospel of Christ, his death and resurrection, duly witnessed and on the strength of this the promise of the forgiveness of sins. All in the room, men and women, responded with warmth, and as a result the Holy Spirit of God came upon them as on the twelve apostles at Pentecost, race made no difference whatsoever. What does this say to us? Surely that the prime task of the Christian Church is to preach the Gospel of the Lord Jesus Christ. This will bring to birth, as nothing else can, fellowship and community and above all life, for the Spirit is the Lord and giver of life. And where there is life there is growth.

At the present time when we look around we cannot surely be blind to the fact that it is the Pentecostal Churches that are showing the most remarkable growth. We may not like their non-liturgical form of worship, their popular hymn-singing and their hand-clapping, some of which has its origin anyway in national temperament, but we ought not to turn a deaf ear to what they are saying: that it is the Spirit who gives life and growth; organization and structures are not primary.

* * *

I have spent my time and your time in this sermon on emphasizing God the Holy Spirit as God in action in our world now. It is not a dead theoretical subject, but a live practical one as relevant now as ever it was. And secondly I have drawn your attention to the Holy Spirit's essential connexion with the Church founded at Pentecost. Time and your patience have forbidden me carrying the subject further into God the Holy Spirit as the Creator, God the Holy Spirit as the Inspirer, God the Holy Spirit operative in all great works of art, literature and music whether the artists and composers were aware of this or not. The Spirit of God in operation cannot be limited for God cannot be limited. And his sphere is not only the community, but the individual as well. This whole subject is so vast we could be in danger of losing our way in it. This is why I have drawn attention to two fundamentals only: the Spirit as a rushing mighty wind, *ruach*, the Spirit as God in action, creating, making, remaking and inspiring, and secondly the Spirit as the life of the Christian Church. Do not forget Pentecost, the origin of the Church is there and the secret of its continued existence and future is the Holy Spirit.

13

THE SACRAMENT OF BAPTISM

There is one body and one Spirit, just as you were called to the one hope that belongs to your call, one Lord, one faith, one baptism, one God and Father of us all, who is above all and through all and in all.

EPHESIANS 4.4–6 (RSV)

I would like you to imagine for a moment that you are on holiday – what an attractive thought! Apart from reclining in the sun, swimming perhaps and enjoying some games, sightseeing is almost bound to be included. You will visit prominent and ancient buildings in the place and this will mean some churches. Every year literally millions of people look around St Paul's Cathedral, Westminster Abbey and York Minster, but not only those great buildings but humbler village churches as well, which will probably be distinctive in some particulars. Wherever you go, however, into whatever churches you enter, you will always find three prominent furnishings: a font, a pulpit and an altar or holy table. And the first of these you encounter is the font because it is situated just inside the door of entry. It ought to be distinctive in structure and decoration and usually is, especially in ancient churches, and it ought not to be used as a convenient place to deposit church magazines and other pieces of literature. It is there for the ministry of a sacrament, the sacrament of baptism, and it is close to the door of entry into the Church because this is the place where the Christian life begins. It is about baptism in water and in the name of the Holy Trinity that I intend preaching now, because we believe in it. But what do we believe?

1 GOD TAKES THE INITIATIVE

First that God always takes the initiative.

Sometimes people who have got into trouble, perhaps even made a mess of their lives, and are charged with this, will reply 'Well, I didn't ask to be born', and that is true. Not one of us has made himself, herself. There was a time when we did not exist. Apparently God willed us to be, or to put the matter another way, God called us into being, called us out of nothing. We are therefore utterly dependent on him. The only alternative to this is chance, which means of course there is no purpose in our being in this world, a most depressing, crippling concept. We are all flotsam and jetsam, interesting maybe, but no more; bits and pieces found floating. Baptism denies this view of persons utterly, and I am thinking of tiny babies wriggling and squealing. They are not merely bits and pieces of life, the mother knows better than this, and dare I say it, yes, even if the children are born outside marriage, children of unmarried mothers, which is a thousand pities. Always the mother looks on her baby with wonder, every birth is a miracle, God's creative purpose is behind it. This is why the newborn child ought never to be left simply to be washed, dressed and cuddled. Something must be done to show that he/she is not a piece of human flotsam and jetsam. There must be a public recognition that God's will brought this child, yes, this child into being or he/she would not be here at all. That public recognition is baptism. Surely, put like this, it cannot be neglected, and ought never to be refused of a child, not even if the parent or parents cannot really understand all it means and are more than a little hazy about their own faith. Baptism says: this is God's child.

2 AN EFFECTIVE SYMBOL

And now we dig a little deeper in our thinking. We can grasp the idea that none of us asked to be born or to be here in this world at all. In our worst moments when everything seems to be going wrong, as we say, we may regret the fact but here we are and we cannot alter the fact. Now I draw your attention to *the Divine Initiative*. God always acts first. We follow on or refuse to follow on. This is true of our Christian faith. We did not make it, it came to us. And if you tell me you attended some evangelistic campaign where you 'decided for Christ' I will still remind you that you responded to an appeal which someone other than yourself made, and also that other people, not you, arranged the campaign where it became possible for you to respond. And for evangelistic campaign you can substitute church, school, prayer group, even books. No one makes himself a Christian believer. To demonstrate the point is the reason why we always have *to be* baptized. No one can baptize himself or herself. We cannot go up to the font, pour water on ourselves and say 'In the name of the Trinity I baptize myself'. It cannot be done. Baptism therefore testifes to the fact that God always goes before, there is always the Divine initiative working in all sorts of ways and through all sorts of people, but it is always God who is behind what takes place.

Baptism is therefore a symbol of this. It is more, it is an *effective* symbol. It is an instrument. Baptism therefore is a sacrament. It does something to the one who is baptized. It makes the child responsive, which is not to say that he/she is bound therefore to respond to the divine initiative in life. This is not so, but it is noteworthy how naturally a child 'takes to' hearing about God, assisted it would seem by the innate existence of wonder which children possess. Their reaction is not that of an adult – 'This cannot be' – it just is. This is why some Churches assert 'Give us a child until he/she is seven and we shall have him/her for life'. Baptism is the beginning of the Christian life. Children are brought into the faith in baptism.

3 MEMBERSHIP OF CHRIST'S CHURCH

And now a third point. Those who are baptized are introduced into the Christian Church, the sphere of God's grace, and are made members of it by baptism in water and in the name of the Trinity, the two essentials. They are sealed with the Holy Spirit and have their place in that body, the Church, where the Holy Spirit particularly, though not exclusively, works. So the spiritual life which is in them is nourished. There are many and various ways in which the Church assists in its care of the baptized, one of them being the provision of Godparents able and willing to take on this responsibility.

This interpretation of baptism, or something like it, which may be labelled objective, has been the general belief in the Church over the centuries but in recent years it has been questioned and something like a subjective view given in its place in some Churches. What is required here is that there should be evidence of Christian faith before baptism is administered. This of course places a query against infant baptism altogether. A baby is unable to provide evidence of Christian faith, and certainly not of repentance of faith. The norm for baptism is therefore looked for in adult baptism, where there is a conscious and deliberate turning to Christ, a forsaking of sins and a renunciation of evil. The baptism is then the seal of this subjective experience. It is pointed out that in the New Testament this is the picture of baptism as it operated in the early Church. Baptism followed conversion, it did not precede it. If such a hard and fast requirement is not made by those who reject the traditional practice of the baptism of infants, nevertheless a baby will not be accepted for baptism where the parents, and indeed Godparents, have only the haziest notion of the Christian faith altogether, let alone of the meaning of baptism. The baptism will be rejected or at least deferred until a course of instruction has been given. It is not surprising if some parents in this situation feel rebuffed and take the baby elsewhere, if anywhere.

But have not these reformers a case? In the New Testament baptism does follow profession of faith in Christ, it does not precede it. This however was in a missionary situation when the gospel was being preached in lands with a non-Christian culture and environment. There are similar situations in many parts of the world today. This is not the situation however in Britain nor in a great part of Europe where there is a widespread Christian tradition and culture – though a case could be made out for affirming that secularism has taken such a widespread hold at the close of the twentieth century that we do actually live in a missionary situation and so believers' baptism as opposed to the traditional general baptism does make sense. And this argument can be reinforced from the plain observation that numbers of people, maybe large numbers, who were baptized as infants, in later life show little evidence of any Christian discipleship at all; some become evildoers, a few actually notorious. Bluntly speaking then, baptism appears to have had little, if any, effect on them.

I said a moment ago that the norm for baptism in the New Testament is believers' baptism. An exception however is recorded in the book of the Acts of the Apostles, chapter 16, verse 33, and no doubt the number of exceptions grew. It reads 'And he', that is, the Philippian gaoler, seeing that Paul and Silas had not escaped during the earthquake, came to belief in the Lord Jesus, 'washed their wounds and was baptized at once with all his family'. Did you notice that? – 'with all his family'. Are you going to argue that they were all 'grown up'? The gaoler would not be as old as that! No, these children had been brought into the sphere of Christian faith, a faith which was ready to give them the sign that they belonged to God too and in the providence of God might come to know and experience it for themselves. Do we see then here the beginning of general baptism as opposed to believers' baptism even in New Testament times?

There is much more that could be said on this subject of baptism. It could be linked to the Atonement. Did Christ die for the sins of the whole world or only for those who come to the belief that he died for them? That is to ask if there is an objective benefit from Christ's death or only a subjective one. We could ask: what is the role of confirmation? Does it point to an incompleteness in baptism? Whole books are written to discuss these questions. What can be expected of one sermon? Certainly this: baptism must not be treated lightly. Parents ought not to let it slip. It is one of the two basic sacraments of the Church. It is a sign of God's love for us all and more than a sign, it is a means by which we receive the love of God into our souls. God always goes before. This is the divine initiative. We are made responsive. Let us respond then and let us help others to respond too, especially the young, for it is for their safety, their eternal safety, their salvation into eternity. So it is for us all.

14
SACRAMENTAL PRESENCE

During supper he took bread, and having said the blessing he broke it and gave it to them, with the words: 'Take this; this is my body.'

MARK 14.22 (NEB)

My subject for this sermon is the Holy Communion, or to use an alternative title, the Eucharist. It is obvious that this is something in which we firmly believe because in church buildings generally the focal point is a table or altar, often in ornate surroundings, with the pulpit and the lectern prominent but set to the sides. Clearly what this arrangement is saying is that what the Church believes and what it preaches is made *visible and available* by what takes place there.

The essence of course is the setting apart of bread and wine, commodities used for the normal feeding and nourishing of our bodies but consecrated for a special and particular purpose at the table or altar. The action has not been chosen at random nor because it has been judged to be an effective way of presenting the Christian message, but because Jesus 'in the same night that he was betrayed, took bread, broke it, and gave it to his disciples' gathered around a table 'saying, This is my body'; similarly they shared a cup of wine. We cannot say that Jesus did this *in order* to institute a rite, but the Holy Communion certainly has its origin in his action that Thursday night just before he went out into the garden of Gethsemane to be arrested and crucified the next day, Good Friday, as we call it. A more solemn and significant time could hardly be imagined.

1 A MEMORIAL

The Holy Communion, the Eucharist, in the simplest interpretation of it is therefore a memorial service recalling this never-to-be-forgotten event which has something momentous to say about the ministry of Jesus. Central to it is action not words. Bread is taken and broken; wine is taken and poured out; then the bread and the wine are shared by those gathered at the table. So the Eucharist can be called *a drama* in the simplest terms of the Lord's ministry through death, also a thankful remembrance by each individual who partakes of what that sacrificial death means. It also brings the partakers together in a close spiritual fellowship. The service therefore is a Eucharist, a thanksgiving, it is also a Holy Communion, all of which means that it is much more than a memorial of what took place that Thursday night (Maundy Thursday), it *does* something for those who share in it.

2 A SYMBOL

And now we are approaching a greater depth if not complexity. The Eucharist is a sacrament. That is a word which, being technical, is inclined to put people off. The dictionary defines it as an outward and visible sign of an inward and spiritual grace. There are everyday examples of this sacramental principle. Here is a girl who in a fit of anger has tossed her wedding ring into the dustbin. Does this matter much? A few pounds will have 'gone west' of course, but is that the real concern? It is that what the ring signifies, and has even at least contributed to making, namely a marriage between two persons, is being broken . . . Or take the case of a flag. You see someone tearing it down from a prominent flagpole. Is that important? A flag in itself is only a piece of coloured cloth, but it signifies patriotism, loyalty, possession and much else besides. The importance of a sacrament lies therefore in what it signifies or, to put the matter another way, of what it is a symbol.

3 AN INSTRUMENT

But is a sacrament only a symbol? Is it not also in some way an instrument, that is to say, does it not accomplish something, has it not an effect on those who employ it or use it? Take a non-religious example again, the case of a national flag. Here is a man who has been exiled in a foreign country at a time of war for a decade; the war has come to an end, his imprisonment is over. Then someone manages to run up his national flag. Are you going to tell me that symbol does nothing to him? He may jump for joy, he may break down in floods of tears because of the memories it stirs up within him. This surely is the point: that flag is not only a visible symbol, it is an instrument. It does something for the one who sees it.

So now we are able to separate out three ways of understanding the Eucharist. It is a memorial of what Jesus did that night before his crucifixion; this is prominent when it is called the Lord's Supper. It is also a symbol of something much more significant and deeper than itself. And then thirdly it is an instrument for the benefit of those who come to partake of it. So then three views – memorial, symbol, effective instrument. To some extent they overlap but the differences are sharp enough to cause division among Christians, not least in what is obvious to even the casual observer, namely High Church and Low Church.

4 THE QUESTION OF HOW

What is at stake here is not simply a matter of taste or aesthetic appreciation. Some Christian worshippers are assisted in their devotions by ritual, others are not, though ritual cannot be avoided altogether for, as I have already said, the Eucharist is essentially a drama, a dramatic presentation of what God in Christ has done for us and continues to do. But the question is *how*: how are the elements, the bread and the wine instruments for the spiritual nourishment of those who partake of them? There are two extremes of belief here. At one end the belief that the duly consecrated elements convey in themselves spiritual nourishment for the partakers, for they are the body and blood of Christ. At the other end the belief that the elements even after consecration convey nothing by themselves, being still bread and wine; such spiritual nourishment as the communicants receive is conditioned by the way in which they receive it, whether in faith that they are in contact with the presence of the living Christ himself or in merely perfunctory attendance on an ecclesiastical ceremony however memorable. The one extreme may include transubstantiation, that is the actual changing of the elements into the body and blood of Christ, or modifications of that belief; the other extreme is called receptionism. Each looks askance at the other. In the one case the concept of instrument dominates the interpretation, in the other the concept of symbol and nothing more.

5 THE PREVENIENT GOD

Now I want to emphasize that devout souls have been nourished, are nourished, in both of these views of the sacrament, that is in the Roman Mass and in the Low Church Lord's Supper, but what I wish to ask is: cannot we approach the Holy Communion without this polarization? I believe we are able and if at this point I speak in personal terms I cannot do otherwise. I can only tell you what the sacrament means to me. I can only tell you what I believe. This is that Christ takes the duly consecrated elements in the Eucharist *and he, not the communicant*, makes them into effective signs of his presence; they then become instrumental in making his presence real there at the altar and at the communion rail, and when we receive the bread and the wine we receive him into our hearts and souls. The receiving is important. We do not ask for anything. We do not theologize. We do not argue. We simply receive but the receiving does not *make* his presence, however replete it may be with faith, his presence is there because of God's action, because he chooses to take up the bread and wine for this purpose. We can of course receive what is offered unworthily. God does not force himself on us. We may not wish for his presence. But he makes the first move. His action, his attitude precedes ours. He is the prevenient God, he goes before, there is always the divine initiative – I am sorry I am using big words, it is because I am struggling to maintain the vital truth, that in the Holy Communion God is acting, the service is not a *mere* symbol.

Of course the Holy Communion is not the only place where the real presence of God is experienced, but it is special, it is unique because Jesus on 'the same night that he was betrayed took bread, broke it and gave it to his disciples, and said "Do this in remembrance of me" ', so we are told in the New Testament. And down through the centuries Christian *have done this* and the Christ who was present in the upper room that night has come to them as the risen glorified one, bringing peace and life and fellowship. I said it is not the only place for realizing in experience a real presence of God. Have you not felt on some mountain top, as you have surveyed the panoramic scene before you, the presence of God? Have you not felt it when you have encountered some saintly person who has given his/her whole life in the service of others? Have you not felt it when someone has opened up to you some passage of Scripture? One of my favourite New Testament stories is that in St Luke, chapter 24, where two disciples of Jesus are pictured as walking out from Jerusalem to a village called Emmaus. They were utterly depressed because the debacle of Good Friday, as they saw it, was eating into their very beings. And then a third figure joined them and opened up to them as they walked what the Scriptures had to say concerning the sufferings of the Messiah. They did not know who he was, but when they reached their destination and all three sat down for their evening meal and the stranger broke bread, they recognized him, he was the risen Christ, his real presence. When they told what had happened to the other disciples gathered in Jerusalem they said 'Did not our hearts burn within us while he talked to us in the way while he opened up the Scriptures?'

Yes, the real presence is experienced in the breaking of bread and with the opening up of the Scriptures. Christ comes in the sacrament and he comes in the ministry of the word. Always he takes the lead.

15
THE BIBLE

Also I heard the voice of the Lord, saying, Whom shall I send, and who will go for us? Then said I, Here am I; send me.

ISAIAH 6.8

In another sermon I invited the hearers to imagine they were on holiday – an attractive thought! It conjures up pictures of relaxation, games perhaps, sport, time spent with the family and friends, and very probably sightseeing, and this may well include looking into churches. There, in addition to striking architecture and stained glass windows, three other characteristics will be noted. First a font, just inside the door of entry, then the altar or holy table very prominent, if not eye-catching, at the east end of the building, then the lectern with a large Bible on it, obviously set there for public reading in worship. If it is a Church of England church, the lectern will probably be placed a little to one side; if some other Protestant denomination, then the Bible will be set on the pulpit, the focal point of the building. What all this says is that the Bible is of fundamental importance in Christian worship. It is as impossible to conceive of a church without a Bible as to think of it without a font or altar, indeed what goes on in the Church is summed up in the phrase 'the ministry of the Word (capital W) and sacraments'. But how is the Word ministered? How are we to think of the Bible? A compendium of Christian doctrine? A source book about religious history? A textbook on ethics? In short, what is the Bible? This is the subject of this sermon.

1 WHAT THE BIBLE IS NOT

First of all I want to stress that the Bible is not a manual of Christian behaviour, that is to say you cannot in any given situation look up the answer to what you should do. Yes, there are a few straightforward prohibitions like 'Thou shalt do no murder', 'Thou shalt not steal', but what about killing in time of war? What about stealing medicine for someone who is dying? The Jews made a monumental attempt to make the Torah, their law, into a book of rules of conduct. There were so many exceptions, however, dependent on circumstances that they had to supplement it with the Mishnah, and before long so many more exceptions that they had to supplement the Mishnah with the Talmud, and so many rules and so many exceptions that there had to be a body of legal experts competent to interpret them and apply them. They were called Scribes. Jesus had nothing in common with their approach, indeed the Scribes and he were in opposite camps. No, the Bible is not a manual of Christian conduct.

Is the Bible then a book of religious history, Jewish and Christian? It certainly is. No one is able to understand the Jewish people, their religion and their customs without consulting, indeed studying the Bible. And this is equally true of the Christian religion. I go further: our knowledge of the historical Jesus – what he said, what he did, what manner of person he was – is almost non-existent apart from the New Testament. In short we are utterly dependent on the Bible for the knowledge of how our faith came into being. So the Bible is a kind of indispensable history book. I say 'kind of' because much of it is in story form, telling of people, what they did, said and what happened to them; indeed this is part of its peculiar attraction. And all is set down in a captivating literary style, not lost even in translation. Once again, however, I have to say the Bible is not primarily a history book setting out the origins of the Jewish and Christian religions.

Is the Bible then a textbook of religious doctrine, Christian doctrine? Are we to find out here exactly what we are to believe and what we are to preach? And again the answer is no. Why do you think the Christian Church laboured – and I mean laboured almost with blood, sweat, toil and tears – to formulate what are called the Catholic creeds? Precisely because the Bible does not provide its readers with a tidy set of authentic doctrines, it is not that sort of book. And when the Churches up to the year AD 415 finalized the creeds, the purpose was to safeguard the Christian faith in Jesus Christ as Lord from what would have become destructive theories about him. The creeds could almost be said to set out what was not to be believed. No, the Bible is not a doctrinal textbook.

2 WHAT THE BIBLE IS

What then is the Bible? The Bible is a book about God, it is a book about the experience of God, men's and women's experience of God, written down by human hands. God neither wrote the Bible nor dictated it. And it tells of the experience of God *in this world* where men and women rub shoulders with other men and women, where good deeds are done and dreadful deeds are done, where there is love and hatred, murder, fornication and double-dealing, but also glimpses of heaven, sublime and beautiful where the clouds break as they do now and again. So the Bible does not stand out there away from us. It issues from the midst of life, earthly life, our life where God has been and is encountered. It tells of these encounters in picture story after picture story, and it is here that we can hear the Word of God for ourselves, 'Word' in this context meaning 'God making himself known'.

These picture stories describe disclosure experiences in life when for a moment in someone's experience time seems to stand still and another dimension is perceived, sometimes dimly, sometimes vividly. Perhaps the most famous in the Bible is Isaiah, chapter 6.

> In the year that king Uzziah died I saw also the Lord sitting upon a throne, high and lifted up; and his train filled the temple. Above it stood the seraphim: each one had six wings; with twain he covered his face, and with twain he covered his feet, and with twain he did fly. And one cried unto another, and said, Holy, holy, holy, is the Lord of hosts; the whole earth is full of his glory. And the posts of the door moved at the voice of him that cried, and the house was filled with smoke. Then said I, Woe is me! for I am undone; because I am a man of unclean lips, and I dwell in the midst of people of unclean lips; for mine eyes have seen the King, the Lord of hosts.

One would have to be made of stone or utterly deaf to language not to sense that this is inspired writing. It is inspired not because of its literal accuracy in describing an event (though this may be so) but because it lifts the reader out of himself, herself, up to a level so way beyond the ordinary and commonplace that we feel ourselves in the divine presence. The language, the literary style and the form of words have contributed to this sensation and as a result we can but account it as *inspired writing*. The Bible is not the only place where inspired writing is encountered. All great literature, poetry and drama has this 'out of the world' quality but because these picture stories in the Bible, some more arresting than others, tell of the experience of God, they are inspired in a unique sense.

3 HOW THE BIBLE SHOULD BE READ

Now it must be admitted that there is a subjective element in this matter of Biblical inspiration. The writing is indeed objectively inspired but it *becomes* inspirational to the reader (or hearer of it when it is read aloud) by what is brought to it by way of spiritual sensitivity and attention. It is not for nothing therefore that the Bible is read in church in the presence of the believing, praying and worshipping community. It is there that the Bible *becomes*, note the word 'becomes', the Word of God. It also becomes the Word of God to the individual in his/her time of personal devotion. Prayer is the proper accompaniment to Bible reading. Scholarship has its proper, I would say indispensable, part to play, but it is not primary. The Bible is a book about God, and the wonder, indeed miracle, is that we can hear God speaking to us through its pages, as we bring our needs, hopes, fears and aspirations, and our faith, into his presence and the needs too of our fellow men and women.

If all this is true about the Bible then it must be read in church during the course of public worship as an inspired set of documents, not all at the same level of inspiration but nevertheless way beyond the pedestrian. The reading of the Bible in church is the ministry of the Word. It must be treated as such and not as a boring legal document and not used as a mere tool for providing a member of the congregation with something to do. And for fear of misunderstanding let me be quick to add, lay people can accomplish the ministry of the Word at the lectern with real effect. I have sat entranced on occasions of such readings, the Bible did indeed *become* the Word of God for me that day. So when next you go sightseeing in a church, notice the lectern as well as the font and the altar, and hope and pray that a real ministry is conducted there.

I come to the closing words of that section from Isaiah, chapter 6. 'Also I heard the voice of the Lord, saying, Whom shall I send, and who will go for us? Then said I, Here am I; send me.' The Word of God when it comes to us is not simply for our education, entertainment, or even spiritual edification, it expects a response. 'Whom shall I send, and who will go for us?' There is a challenge in it. We are expected to think differently and to act differently. No one who grasps this will ever count the reading of lessons in church as a subsidiary activity, it can change lives, it may be revolutionary, certainly stimulate the spirits of the hearers. Don't bypass the lectern in church, the Word of God is active there and it can be 'sharper than any two-edged sword'.

16
WHAT IS MAN?

When I look at thy heavens, the work of thy fingers, the moon and the stars which thou hast established; what is man that thou art mindful of him, and the son of man that thou dost care for him?

PSALM 8.3, 4 (RSV)

A few days ago my eye was caught by the reproduction of a blurred photograph in the newspaper, blurred because snapshot surreptitiously. It wasn't meant to be seen. It depicted a column of shabby men shuffling along obviously under duress. The wording under the picture told us they were political prisoners in China, of whom there were many large numbers held in secret.

The category of political prisoner is one of which we have heard much in the twentieth century. It is the modern form of slavery, and slavery it certainly is. Slavery has existed since the world began, often on a vast scale. It was the horrible underside to the achievements of the great civilizations of antiquity. Those stupendous pyramids in Egypt were erected in the cruellest conditions by myriads of slaves. And those buildings that characterize classical Greece and Rome which we rightly admire were likewise the work of slaves under the lash. These taskmasters had no conscience about using men and women in this way, they called them 'living tools', men and women of no value except the use to which they could be put. Of intrinsic worth in themselves they had none. And you say to me 'Oh well, all that is past and gone'. Is it? What about the blurred picture in the newspaper a few days ago?

I am saying all this not to produce horror stories but to introduce the question: what is man? And of course I include women. If he shouldn't be treated as 'a living tool', why not?

What do we believe about man? What do we preach? This is my subject for this sermon.

1 TWO INCOMPLETE ANSWERS

The elementary answer to this question is that man is a kind of superior animal. That is to say he has an affinity with nature, is part of the natural order. He breathes, endlessly seeks for food, mates, rears a family like the animals, is active, often violently so, for weeks, months or years, even decades, then dies. Man is a creature alongside many other and varied creatures. We bear witness to this fact when we say about someone 'he likes his creature comforts'. And yet he is different, markedly different, he has evolved differently. The question therefore arises, 'What makes him different?' 'What makes him unique?' The most ready answer given to this question is *reason*. Man is separate from all other creatures because he alone has reason. And over the centuries it has developed to a fantastic degree of ingenuity and competence, most obvious perhaps in the realm of science and technology. Man therefore is a rational creature set apart from all other creatures by his obvious faculty of reason.

But will this answer suffice? Is not man more than reason? Is he not able to stand outside his reason, even to discuss it? Clearly therefore he transcends reason. What governs him is more complex than reason alone. If I may introduce a personal note here, I was for many years in close contact with the personnel of one of the foremost scientific institutions in the country, and what I observed was how unsatisfying alone the pursuit of pure science was found to be; in considerable numbers they sought relief in music. Yes, man is certainly distinguishable in the world of nature by his reason, but this is not the whole answer to the question 'what is man?' There is something else about him.

And if reason were the determining factor which made man what he is, what is to be thought or done about the masses in whose lives reason plays a very insignificant part? Some because they lack the faculty for it, and vastly many more because the impoverishment of their condition of existence makes it virtually impossible, they can only barely keep themselves alive. These are the people whom the more fortunate down through the ages have called 'living tools', men and women of no intrinsic worth in themselves, people ripe for slavery. So what is man? It is not a mere academic question.

2 MAN IS MADE IN THE IMAGE OF GOD

What then do we believe? What do we preach about the nature of man? We believe and we preach that the nature of man can only be understood in relation to God. If we do not believe in God, whatever our protestations about the remarkable achievements of reason on the part of man, he will be underestimated, his intrinsic worth discounted if he cannot be useful, that is, be 'a living tool'; he may even be 'liquidated' to use a modern phrase. In general the harsh treatment of our fellow men has been perpetrated when belief in God is either non-existent or distorted. It is evident therefore that belief in God saves man, and I am not now talking about eternal salvation.

Now our belief about the nature of man is summed up in the phrase 'Man is made in God's image'. Obviously this does not refer to his physical form because God has none; he has no physical body, so let me elaborate. The origin of our belief is in Genesis, chapter 1, verse 27: 'So God created man in his own image; in the image of God created he him; male and female created he them.' Man therefore (and the verse is specific in including women as equal) is *the creation of God.* Whatever way we understand evolution, and we cannot deny it, man is not merely the product of it. He is God's creation; even more, he is the crown of God's creative action. Genesis, chapter 1 marks a distinct order of creation: first the heaven, then earth, then plant life, then countless living creatures.

There follows a break in the narrative so as to place man in a class by himself. 'Then God said, "Let us make man in our image and likeness to rule the fish in the sea, the birds of heaven, the cattle, all wild animals on earth and all reptiles that crawl upon the earth". So God created man in his own image; in the image of God created he them, male and female he created them.' Man, therefore, according to the Bible is unique, he is the creation of God, different from all the other created creatures because in his case he is like God. God is the pattern by which we are to estimate what is man's nature.

I have already said that this likeness to God cannot refer to physical form. God has no physical form, God is not a body. Nor will it suffice to say that, different from the animals, man is able to think. The unique fact about man is that he is able to choose, choose what he will do, even what he will be; he has therefore some faculty by which he is able to stand outside himself. He has freedom from necessity: so much so that he can even reject belief in God who created him. This we can call *the spirit or the soul of man*. It is here that man is like God. Only in the light of relationship can the nature of man be understood. Take away belief in God altogether and man, and mankind is left as an enigma.

I have been referring to man's soul, that which makes him unique; let me now refer to his body. In the culture in which Christianity grew up, that is, the Greco-Roman, and let us remember it was quite remarkable, the human body was thought little of. I do not mean no Greek or Roman, certainly in society, made use of cosmetics or took trouble over their appearance. This was not so, quite the reverse, but the body was a temptation, a liability, it distracted the mind, it was the enemy of higher thoughts and noble living. In itself therefore the body was reckoned to be worthless, something to be despised, indeed fit for burial – its final destiny. Now Christianity based on the Bible will have none of this. Man is the creation of God and as in the Genesis chapter already referred to, the very first chapter of the Bible, the creation of God is pronounced as 'very good'. Man's body is not to be despised. It contributes to what he is, and what he is contributes to his body. Man's nature therefore in its wholeness is of infinite worth. This is what we believe. This is what we preach.

3 BODY AND SOUL

And so we do not believe and preach a kind of dualism: we have mortal bodies but we have immortal souls. Our gospel is a gospel of the resurrection of the person, not of the immortality of the soul. We shall not be souls without bodies in the life after death. We shall have a resurrection body, a vehicle for the life of the soul. The soul survives the death of the body. Anyone who has been a witness at a deathbed scene senses this. 'He/she has left us' is the most frequent comment. There is a permanence about the soul or spirit of a person *in this life* which the body does not possess. The body undergoes many changes or mutations in the course of a normal life, it is the soul that gives the person his/her distinctive character and unity. This survives death and is given a resurrection body raised up from the body that has died, a new vehicle for the soul.

Is this that I am saying hard to grasp? Of course it is. But does not St Paul point to this in 2 Corinthians 5.1–5, which the New English Bible translation has clarified?

> For we know that if the earthly frame that houses us today should be demolished, we possess a building which God has provided – a house not made by human hands, eternal, and in heaven. In this present body we do indeed groan; we yearn to have our heavenly habitation put on over this one – in the hope that, being thus clothed, we shall not find ourselves naked. We groan indeed, we who are enclosed within this earthly frame; we are oppressed because we do not want to have the old body stripped off. Rather our desire is to have the new body put on over it, so that our mortal part may be absorbed into life immortal. God himself has shaped us for this very end; and as a pledge of it he has given us the Spirit.

What are the supports for this glimpse into our future beyond the veil? and it is no more than a glimpse, and shadowy at that, but the supports are firm. There are two: the Incarnation, that is the Word of God taking human flesh in a recognizable body, Jesus of Nazareth, and secondly that body raised from the dead. This is where our gospel is based, our good news, a message to be proclaimed worldwide for every man, yes even that forced labourer in a foreign land for whom no one seems to care, yes even for him, certainly for him, something to sing about. God cares for him, even into eternity.

We have a gospel to proclaim,
good news for men in all the earth;
The gospel of a Saviour's name:
We sing his glory, tell his worth.

Edward J. Burns

17

MAN IS A SINNER

God was in Christ reconciling the world to himself, no longer holding men's misdeeds against them, and that he has entrusted us with the message of reconciliation. We come therefore as Christ's ambassadors.

2 CORINTHIANS 5.19, 20

As we look back over our national life during the last twelve months I wonder what you would say have been the main preoccupations. There has been the Irish question of course, but this is now of many years' standing. There is the misery of what we used to call Yugoslavia. There is the national debt and the imposition of heavier taxation. There is redundancy and unemployment, hurtful to many thousands of people. But something else has raised its head, an ugly head, in a way unexpectedly and suddenly, a widespread concern about the apparent decay of moral standards in the community: the difference between right and wrong is not accepted, the general philosophy seems to be 'Get what you can while you can' and never mind the consequences.

Explanations are offered for this state of affairs: the educational system, the breakdown of marriage and home life, unemployment, inadequate housing. Undoubtedly there is truth in these suggested reasons, but the awkward query is: if these defects could be remedied and that speedily, would the present sorry situation be done away? Is not the root of the trouble in people, not in circumstances however much they may aggravate it? To say this is not popular and will arouse the charge of callousness about people's misfortunes, even leading to anger. No true Christian however is indifferent to the troubles and pains of his fellow men and women, indeed Christians are in the forefront in unselfishly seeking to bring relief, but they have to confess to this basic belief that man though made in the image of God is a sinner. It may be unpalatable but it is true and we know it.

1 MAN IS A SINNER

Now what does this mean to say that man is a sinner? Does it mean that he/she commits certain specific sins: fraud, lying, bullying, sexual harassment, stealing and so on. Yes, it does, but if we are not guilty of any of these, or any other specific sins like them, we could reckon that we are not sinners, and that is not true. These are symptoms of an underlying fault in human nature which may show itself in various forms, some more horrendous than others, most perhaps less obvious than others, but damaging all the same. To confess (if we do) that we are sinners refers primarily to what we are, not to what we do or have done. We are people who want to go our own way, and protest 'Why shouldn't we?'. We have our freedom and we wish to keep it, why should we be beholden to anybody else? Let us each one 'do his/her own thing'. We are all agreed, let us demonstrate it by our independence. We don't want tradition, class distinction, racial prejudice or anything else or anybody else to stand in our path. Let each and all go his or her own way without any deference to anyone else. This is how we think because we are sinners. We can manage our own lives, thank you very much, with no interference from anyone else – and here comes the sharp point, no interference from God or cramping belief in God. Let us be free, gloriously free. This is the way to happiness, this is the way of achievement, each one managing his own, her own life as he/she will. It is however a delusion, being the root of sin, that is, rebellion nourished by personal pride, aggressive pride, and it goes before a fall.

2 THE HUMAN PARADOX

Now we are touching on what I will call the paradox in man. From what I have been saying you might believe that man, being a sinner, is rotten through and through, but that is not so. I have already preached a sermon on the nature of man derived from the Bible in which is set out the belief that man is made in God's image. How can this be if he be rotten through and through? This would be a ridiculous assertion. The artists, the poets, the musicians, the sculptors, the literary men and women have left behind and still produce marvels of truth, beauty and goodness, and they cannot all be classed as religious people, let alone Christians, not a few indeed would call themselves agnostics or atheists, but out of their natures have come many wonderful things. Man, I repeat, is a paradox; he is made in the image of God but he is also a sinner. And this is the nature of his sin: his power of self-determination, that is, his capacity to choose what he will do and what he will achieve, turns into self-centredness which invariably becomes selfishness, sometimes gross. Self is in the centre of his picture. What he wants, what he can win for himself, what praise or adulation he can bask in. To put the matter in everyday language, 'Number One is the centre of his world', and then there is no room for God or very little room. God does not 'come into the picture', he is dethroned, indeed he has never been recognized as on the throne, man is the master of all things, there is no one else. And what man has mastered, the conquest of space is a case in point, is impressive. In view of all the human achievement, the hurt is the awareness that it has not produced happiness or even contentment on the part of man, disillusionment stalks the earth. Why is this? Not because man is rotten but because he is a rebel, on strike against the very idea of God with a right to any kind of say in his life, and no consciousness of the will of God to be accepted. This is the tragedy of man, misdirected goodness in some rare cases so blatant that he has to be called half-angel, half-devil.

Here then is the human problem – *can man save himself?* He thinks he can. Of course he does. He always, or almost always, places himself at the centre of his picture, indeed he would complain that there is no one else to put there. Man has to look after himself. In that world of self-centredness however, which rapidly develops into selfishness, man becomes a lost soul. This is the plight of the sinner.

3 THE WAY OF SALVATION

If man is unable to save himself, is there then a way of salvation? The Bible answers this question in the affirmative. The heart of the matter is what St Paul wrote to the Philippians (2.5–11):

> Let your bearing towards one another arise out of your life in Jesus Christ. For the divine nature was his from the first; yet he did not think to snatch at equality with God, but made himself nothing, assuming the nature of a slave. Bearing the human likeness, revealed in human shape, he humbled himself, and in obedience accepted even death – death on a cross. Therefore God raised him to the heights and bestowed on him the name above all names, that at the name of Jesus every knee should bow – in heaven, on earth, and in the depths – and every tongue confess, 'Jesus Christ is Lord', to the glory of God the Father. (NEB)

Jesus is the prime example of breaking out of the trap of self-centredness. 'He made himself nothing' or, as the Authorized Version of the Bible has it, 'He made himself of no reputation'. It is not enough however to show man the way, he needs rescuing before he can begin to go that way, let alone keep on it. And so Jesus appears on the world scene not only as the example, indeed not primarily as the example, but as the Saviour. It is on the cross, an ignominious death, that he is the Saviour. Because of this he is raised to the heights and bestowed with the name above all names, at which every knee should bow confessing, not himself, but Jesus Christ as Lord to the glory of God the Father. This is the way out of self-centredness, the root of our human woes, setting Christ on the throne, Christ the Saviour.

The modern fashion is to attribute everything about our personality and our condition either to our genes or to our environment. We cannot help being what we are. Responsibility is sloughed off. The Bible will have none of this. It does not reduce man and woman to automata. We have 'erred and strayed' like lost sheep, as the Book of Common Prayer has it, a penetrating observation, for it recognizes that what plays a large part in man's sinfulness is not downright wickedness but sheer stupidity. Nevertheless man is lost and is guilty for his condition. It is possible that we can endure to be called sinners, after all we are all 'in the boat' together, but what we resent is being labelled *guilty* sinners. It is not our fault that we are as we are. But the Bible does not give way, and our services of worship that are true to it call for penitence at that very outset, humble penitence, penitence on our knees. But forgiveness is the response, God's forgiveness, pardon and forgiveness for all our sins. This is possible not because God is 'soft on wrong-doing' but because in Christ he came where man the sinner is and, as it were, stood beside him sharing the consequences of his guilty rebellion. So God sees us not alone but in the company of Christ by his will and loving purpose. He is our Advocate, he, the guiltless one, is our representative, he is this for the whole world, if we will have him (1 John 2.1).

So the complex sorry state of man, created in God's image but also a sinner, is provided for by the Grace of God. This is what we believe, this is what we preach. It is why we have a gospel to proclaim. We have a Saviour, Jesus Christ the Lord. As St Paul wrote in his letter to the Corinthians (5.19, 20 NEB): 'God was in Christ reconciling the world to himself, no longer holding men's misdeeds against them, and that he has entrusted us with the message of reconciliation. We come therefore as Christ's ambassadors.'

18

THE HUMAN PREDICAMENT

God shows his love for us in that while we were yet sinners Christ died for us.

ROMANS 5.8 (RSV)

Last year a book was published under the title *Night and Fog.* I am sure I could not bear to read it, judging from the extracts included in a review of its contents. The writer is a Dutchman, a former solicitor, who tells his story from what he managed to write on lavatory paper during his years of imprisonment in German concentration camps, ending in Dachau. The one-time Director of the State Institute for War Documentation in Amsterdam says in a foreword that he does not know of any publication 'which records reminiscences so truthful and so striking' as in this book. It communicates the stench of the camps, the faeces and the urine running across the floors, soaking the clothing of the prisoners. Men snatched pieces of bread from the filth of the floor and ate them. Conditions were worse in Dachau. Mud half-a-metre deep, the only clothes allowed in the freezing cold were underclothes and pyjamas, everything covered with lice. Water pipes and drainage unknown. One day the prison guard put some twenty walking skeletons under the showers and turned on boiling water, watching them scalded and dying on the floor, and on another day setting their dogs on the prisoners to tear large chunks of flesh away.

No, I couldn't read it, and I wonder if after fifty years from the date of all this happening the book ought to have been published. This however is the frightening question: are horrors such as this all over and done with now? But what savagery is going on at present in the former Yugoslavia, not to mention countries virtually untouched by European civilization? How can people stoop to such beastliness? What are human beings made of that they can outstrip the animals in cruelty? This is a subject I have already touched on in my sermon 'What is the nature of man?' but I come back to it. Is man totally depraved? Sometimes so it would appear that he is, 'utterly indisposed, disabled and made opposite to all good, and wholly inclined to evil', as one theological statement describes him. But surely we cannot believe this. What then do we believe about the nature of man? What do we take for granted? What do we assume? What do we preach?

1 MAN IS A CONTRADICTION

First then let me re-emphasize that man, and I include woman, is a contradiction. He is good and he is bad. He can rise to heights of impressive nobility and he can sink to depths of revolting foulness. He can create works of surpassing beauty and he can invent instruments of diabolical cruelty. Illustrations are superfluous. We know the case only too well. How then do we account for the evil? Is it due to ignorance? To a lack of education? To the influence of upbringing? To the genes which we inherit? To the environment? A more pressing question is: what can be done to strengthen the good in men and curtail the evil? It has pressed on the human race since it struggled above the level of barbarism. It is still the perpetual problem of civilization, which at the best of times is fragile. It has been talked about in Britain in the last twelve months because in some sections of the community any difference between right and wrong seems unknown. Will then the evil in man gradually outstrip the good in him? How can these dire consequences be avoided? This is the question facing Western civilization at the close of the twentieth century. There is an urgency about it.

2 MAN IS A SINNER

The second point I want to make is that man is a sinner and it is for his eventual well-being to recognize the fact. Sin of course is a religious word. To talk of sin makes no sense if God does not exist or if his existence is not recognized. A sinner is someone who stands in the presence of God, ultimately deriving his very life from God, but who does not recognize this. And since God is made known to us in the person of Jesus Christ, sin is that in our lives which does not square with Jesus Christ. We recoil from this statement. We might be ready to admit that we are sinners if we juggle with people's pension funds to replenish our own purses, or if we go out soliciting on the streets at night, or deliberately stand in the way of someone's chances of promotion in a business. And because we do not involve ourselves in these lurid misdemeanours we reckon we are not sinners, not bad sinners anyway. As soon however as we concede that sin is all that in our lives which does not square with the pattern of behaviour revealed in the true man Jesus of Nazareth, we know our defences are down, we are sinners all of us. Not all alike, no, not equally culpable, but sinners, we fall short of what we should be. This is the truth about all men and women to whatever race, culture or class they, no, we, may belong. We stand in the presence of God as sinners.

We do not like this assessment. It is humiliating. We are by nature proud. We like to be masters of our own destiny. We look down on people who have not achieved what we have achieved in life. We set ourselves up above our fellows, each according to his or her predilections. Accomplished and capable people who are also humble are rare and even they can be proud of their humility. We are loath to admit that the skills we possess are a gift in the first place from God, however much we may have advanced them subsequently. Yes, I am labouring this universality of human sinfulness, but it is not a quirk of mine. It is a basic belief of the Christian Church. This is what we believe, and this is why in our services of public worship almost before we have begun we get down on our knees – oh how humiliating to confess to God that 'we have erred and strayed from thy ways like lost sheep. We have followed too much the devices and desires of our own hearts' (BCP) or, in these alternative words, 'Almighty God, our heavenly Father, we have sinned against you and against our fellow men, in thought and word and deed, through negligence, through weakness, through our own deliberate fault' (ASB). Is this morbid? Is it psychologically unhealthy? Why does the Church harp on our human sinfulness? It is because our sins stand in the way of our access to God and only in fellowship with him can we be what we might be. Our sinfulness, product of our nature, and our wilfulness, has to be dealt with before we can rise to the possibilities open to us.

3 MAN IS UNABLE TO RESCUE HIMSELF

And now thirdly this. We cannot get clear of our sinfulness by our own efforts. Sinners, in the nature of the case, cannot stop being sinners. We cannot 'pull ourselves up by our own bootlaces', or, in the more dignified language of Jeremiah, 'Can the Ethiopian change his skin or the leopard his spots?' (Jeremiah 13.23). We are by nature sinners. Sin is endemic in us. We cannot shake it off nor outgrow it, nor neutralize it by balancing good works. We have to be rescued. We cannot rescue, we cannot save ourselves. This is the human predicament. But God himself has provided the lifeline, God has come where we are in the world, into the beauty and into the filth. God has become man, not only thereby showing what we could be and how far we fall short of this possibility, but also to show himself as the Saviour, the Rescuer from our predicament. This is what the Incarnation we celebrate at Christmas – 'And the Word was made flesh, and dwelt among us' (John 1.14) – is all about. This is the beginning of the Gospel, the beginning of the good news.

Now there is a view that the Incarnation is itself God's saving act for mankind. The idea is that in assuming human flesh God purified it of its innate imperfections which could not be removed by self-effort. This is not however the view which has predominated in Christendom, certainly not in Western Christendom. Furthermore it does not accord with the predominance given in the New Testament to the cross of Christ, first in the narrative sections, that is the gospels, but also in the epistles which draw out the implications of the cross. The crucifixion of Jesus does not only and chiefly stand as a ghastly illustration of the cruelty of human nature at its worst, a cruelty committed over and over again in history ancient and modern, as in the account of the concentration camps with which I opened this sermon. The crucifixion of Jesus Christ was God's way of unblocking our access to God occasioned by our own endemic human sinfulness. The cross is God's instrument of rescue for all of us, the lifeline to be grasped, and it is the Church's perennial task to draw attention to it. We are asked to bow down and admit that we are sinners, and then grasp the lifeline in the faith that this is God's way for us to begin to be what we might be.

It is inevitable that we should ask how this act of God in the crucifixion of Jesus works. How can a gruesome deed on that execution site outside Jerusalem's walls two thousand years ago affect my standing, our standing before God? Was God's anger at the sins of man propitiated by this sacrifice on the part of Jesus? No, I do not think that this is the explanation, though thousands and thousands of people have been led to trust the lifeline of the cross by it. Is it that seeing the lengths to which God in Christ was willing to go we are lifted up by this example of self-sacrifice to throw off our useless proud self-sufficiency? No, I do not think this psychological example comes anywhere near what was accomplished at Calvary, it is too subjective, though once again it has to be admitted that it has helped many to hold on to the cross who would otherwise have reacted against the propitiation type of explanation. Perhaps we had better see the cross as the place of God's victory over sin for us and in faith leave the explanation there. At the end of the day this is all we can do. Hold on in faith to the cross as the way of rescue for us sinners, humbly admitting that that is what we are. This is what we believe. This is what we preach. The message is compressed in my text from the epistle to the Romans – and I will ask you to notice that everything stems from the love of God – 'God shows his love for us in that while we were yet sinners Christ died for us.'

19
LOVE SUPERSEDES LAW

I tell you, unless you show yourselves far better men than the Pharisees and the doctors of the law, you can never enter the Kingdom of Heaven.

MATTHEW 5.20 (NEB)

The overall title of this collection of sermons is *Preaching What We Believe*. The title was chosen for me and I willingly accepted it, for there does appear to be uncertainty on the part of the general public as to what the Church does believe these days, and haziness on the part of many churchgoers, but I have to admit the title is open to misunderstanding. It could give the impression that the main purpose of preaching is to instil certain beliefs in the minds of the hearers. And some people, perhaps many, mistakenly reckon preaching is telling the hearers 'where to get off'. This is evident from the retort of someone uneasy at the advice being given, and the way it is given, shouting 'Hey, stop *preaching* at me, will you?' The basic reason for preaching however is not to provide information, even religious information though it has its part to play, nor is it to entertain, and certainly preaching should give no place whatsoever to scolding: this is to debase preaching. The purpose of preaching is to inspire the hearers so to live that they enter the Kingdom of heaven. So my text taken from the preaching of Jesus, what is commonly called 'The Sermon on the Mount': 'I tell you, unless you show yourselves far better men than the Pharisees and doctors of the law, you can never enter the Kingdom of heaven.'

1 THE HEART IS WHAT COUNTS

I don't know of course, but my guess is that the disciples squirmed when they heard Jesus say this. Better men than the Pharisees and doctors of the law? Impossible! They knew, they saw the meticulous care with which the Pharisees and doctors of the law sought to put into practice even the details of the Mosaic law entrusted to them. Maybe they did fiddle them a bit, but, they would think, who doesn't fiddle a bit sometimes? Perhaps they did tend to obey the letter of the law and miss out on the spirit of it. But the Pharisees weren't all downright humbugs, we must be fair to them. In an environment of widespread moral decadence they stood for standards and in large measure kept to them.

What on earth did Jesus mean then when he said to his disciples 'Unless you show yourselves far better men than the Pharisees and the doctors of the law, you can never enter the Kingdom of Heaven'? This at least was perfectly clear: Jesus was concerned with the judgement of God on people; not on formulating an ethical ideal, not planning a better social order nor teaching how to make a proper use of the earth's resources, all matters of prior importance in the eyes of the Western world. His attention was fixed on how we stand now, and will stand in the presence of God, and – note this – the Kingdom of God is not only a future inheritance but a present possession. Yes, he was indeed saying that we should live as men and women who one day have to die, and it is well for us to go about our daily activities in the light of it, but the Kingdom of heaven can be experienced *here and now.* We can enter it now or fail to enter it now. It is love, joy, peace, patience, kindness, goodness, faithfulness, gentleness, self-control. And law, rules and regulations about conduct simply do not work in this sphere at all (Galatians 5.22, 23). Entry into the Kingdom of heaven depends entirely on what a person's heart is. This is why Jesus told his disciples that they would never enter the Kingdom of heaven if they attempted to order their lives morning, noon and night like the Pharisees and doctors of the law by means of a rule book where answers to moral problems could be looked up, as it were, by consulting the index. The heart is what counts.

2 THE LAW OF LOVE PARAMOUNT

I can't help wondering if some of the more intelligent and sensitive among the Pharisees didn't reckon all this bondage to rules and regulations, so characteristic of their lives, misguided. Could the number perhaps be slimmed down? Could there perhaps be a revised and simplified code of conduct? I make this suggestion because I read that one day a Pharisee, a lawyer too, put the question to Jesus, 'Teacher, which is the great commandment in the law?' And this is the answer he received. 'You shall love the Lord your God with all your heart, with all your soul and with all your mind. This is the great and first commandment. And a second is like it, You shall love your neighbour as yourself. On these two commandments depend all the law and the prophets.' So the corpus of moral laws was not merely slimmed down, it was replaced with something altogether different, the governing factor is not law but love and love is a sphere where law does not operate. Don't we know? You cannot command people to love. They have to be inspired to it, they have to be moved with the emotions captured.

And now I fancy I can hear someone objecting. You say, Mr Preacher, that Jesus gave no rules about conduct. What about the instructions in the Sermon on the Mount as set out in Matthew 5.39–42? 'If someone slaps you on the right cheek, turn and offer him your left. If a man wants to sue you for your shirt, let him take your coat as well. If a man in authority makes you go one mile, go with him two. Give when you are asked to give; and do not turn your back on a man who wants to borrow.' But these are not rules to be obeyed. As such they could be ludicrous. 'Give when you are asked to give' or, as the Authorized Version, 'Give to everyone that asketh you'. Just as if we could! No, what we have here is illustrations, yes, illustrations of the generosity, or if you like love, that will inspire what action may be taken sometimes and in some situations, when the heart is right, and love of God and of neighbour is the motivating force and not subservience to a rule book.

3 ENTRY INTO THE KINGDOM OF HEAVEN

I come back for a moment to that Pharisee, that lawyer who asked Jesus which is the great and first commandment. And when he received the answer, love of God and love of neighbour, he spoke up (according to St Mark's version) and said 'Well said, Master. You are right in saying that God is one and beside him there is no other. And to love him with all your heart, all your understanding and all your strength, and to love your neighbour as yourself – that is far more than any burnt offerings or sacrifices.' When Jesus saw how sensibly he answered, he said to him 'You are not far from the Kingdom of God'. In the light of this I think this Pharisee, if and when he overheard Jesus say to his disciples 'Unless you show yourselves far better men than the Pharisees and the doctors of the law, you can never enter the Kingdom of heaven', nodded his head, he understood. What we do, what we say, how we behave will only stand up in the presence of God if it is motivated by the heart and not by the rule book, if it derives from the heart and not from a set of ordinances, nor even from dogmas we may feel inclined to preach. Perhaps we need to keep this in the back of our minds in this series of sermons, preaching what we believe.

And now some words which you will recognize:

> I may have faith strong enough to remove mountains; but if I have no love, I am nothing. I may dole out all I possess, or even give my body to be burnt, but if I have no love, I am none the better. Love is patient; love is kind and envies no one. Love is never boastful nor conceited, nor rude; never selfish, nor quick to take offence. Love keeps no score of

wrongs; does not gloat over other men's sins, but delights in the truth. There is nothing love cannot face; there is no limit to its faith, its hope, and its endurance.

That is what St Paul wrote to the people of Corinth, a man who had once lived fiercely by Pharisaic rules and regulations, but on the Damascus road one day he encountered the risen Christ and all that was changed, he knew then that he could not be justified by how assiduously he had kept the Pharisaic law book. None of us will enter the Kingdom of heaven by the high score of good deeds we may have totted up, nor the total of bad deeds we may have avoided. God's method of assessing us has an entirely different basis. It depends on love, love of God, love of neighbour, a disposition of heart and soul that cannot be commanded but can be inspired and is inspired by the life of Jesus and the risen Christ.

4 THE ESSENCE OF PREACHING

This then brings me back to preaching. The essence of preaching is not providing religious information, though it has its part to play, it is not entertaining, it is certainly not scolding, preaching at people. Preaching, Christian preaching is presenting Christ, the historical Jesus and the Christ of spiritual experience, and presenting him in such a way as to inspire. Out of this come faith, hope and love, the characteristics of the truly Christian man and woman. This is how we enter the Kingdom of heaven making us better people than the Pharisees and the doctors of the law. But we love them too, misguided though they may be, we do not ostracize, we do not condemn. The writ for us is to love God and our neighbour as ourselves, everything depends on these two commandments.

20
PROVIDENCE

So it was not you who sent me here, but God; and he has made me a father to Pharaoh, and lord of all his house and ruler over all the land of Egypt.

GENESIS 45.8 (RSV)

In this sermon I am going to talk about Providence. I have preached on this subject but not often, and I guess it is a subject rarely handled in the pulpit. But I believe in it. Most people do, though you wouldn't catch them elaborating on the subject, but somehow it is in people's system. The other day I met a woman well past middle age whose life has been rough, to put it mildly. Broken home, divorce, financial hardship, meagre accommodation, loneliness and unemployment. Then out of the blue a suitable job turned up; even better, she liked her employer. This is what she said, quite half a dozen times, in her simple homely way: 'I think him up there', and she lifted her eyes heavenwards, 'must be looking after me.' Not very theological, I admit, but it represented her 'gut faith' – pardon the phrase – in Providence. And most people have it. This is the striking fact about human nature, indeed only those men and women with no religious feeling whatsoever or a definite antipathy to it are without a rough and ready belief in Providence.

1 PROBLEMS ABOUT PROVIDENCE

I put it this way because there are difficulties. Take first what we call 'natural calamities'. An earthquake, a disastrous flood, an outbreak of some fatal disease. It is the innocent victims that trouble us. How can we believe in God, let alone in Providence which allows people to be caught in the trap of events over which they have no control? And God does nothing or seems to do nothing. But let us think for a moment. For what are we asking? A world in which there is no hardship? A form of existence without pain? A life 'easy-go' all the way? But we can't imagine such a world. It is unrealistic. And aren't the people we admire most those who have battled against unbelievable odds? Every month I see the magazine called *Reader's Digest* produce a story of someone who has overcome dire calamities and risen to a remarkable height of personal stature and acclaim in consequence. Isn't it the truth that if there were no calamities there would be no heroes? And I note this, that not content with the hazards there are in life as we find it, there is no lack of both men and women who specifically court danger. They climb Everest, walk the length of Africa on foot, sail solo around the world. They actually choose to pit their limited strength against the giant strengths of nature to show of what they are made. All of which adds up to this, that we cannot rule out the whole notion of Providence simply on the grounds that in God's creation there are dangers. It is not an argument that will hold.

And now, maybe, you want to come back at me. You want to ask why it is then that pain and natural calamities (so called) become such a problem for us. The answer is, they become a problem when they appear to contribute absolutely nothing to our human welfare but rather the reverse. They crush us as if we were vermin or objects of no particular value. There are calamities which seem to cry aloud that the creation is not the work of a caring God but is one vast mechanism of impersonal cause and effect, a view stimulated by the current popularity of science and technology. So there is seen to be no room for Providence, no place for a God of love, the world is one big relentless machine.

Nor is this all. We human beings seem in any case to be misfits in the world. We struggle and struggle to achieve something and we do achieve something, but never ultimate solutions to life's problems. Always, like mountaineers, when we have scaled one peak, we see further peaks beyond. The truth seems to be that we are condemned to perpetual struggle, always travelling but never arriving; the only certain arrival is death, whatever our effort and however magnificent. If this is what is really meant by the providential ordering of the world, how can we possibly believe it?

Problems and problems then. And I haven't finished. More upsetting than everything is the fact of sheer wickedness in the world. Why did God allow Auschwitz? Why did that man get away with raping his baby daughter till the police caught him? Why did not God fuddle the brains of the scientists when they started work on the atomic bomb? Why? Why? Why? Questions of this order have haunted mankind, pinpointed by the question: Why do the wicked prosper? How can we believe in any purpose in the ordering of the world in the face of all this? It seems to be 'a tale told by an idiot signifying nothing'. Even the Bible takes up the problem in the story of Job and a number of the Psalms.

2 BELIEF IN PROVIDENCE HOLDS ON

This however is the surprising fact that in spite of these devastating assaults on the very idea of Providence, the belief holds on, not merely for a few enlightened Christians but as the gut feeling of the vast mass of ordinary people, muddled no doubt, vague and intermittent, but it holds on. The creation is not a nonsense, somehow there is a purpose at the back of it, though it must be admitted, it lies half hidden as a great mystery.

Why then does the belief in Providence hold on? First and perhaps foremost because of experience. The couple hand-in-hand being interviewed by the vicar about their forthcoming marriage begin by saying 'We feel we were meant for each other'. The man in the hospital bed suddenly taken ill and missing his appointment for a new job says to the chaplain 'Maybe it has all happened for some good purpose'. Even the soldier who did not get hit in the fierce hail of bullets as he charged the enemy: 'I guess no bullet had my number on it.'

Why then does belief in Providence hold on? Because we cannot believe that there is anything in the world more important than a human being, no work of art, no giant piece of intricate machinery, no fresh scientific discovery. What is their ultimate value if men and women do not somewhere, somehow profit by them? And must not this supreme importance of the human also exist in the mind of God? If so, how can we dodge the conviction that the world in all its orderliness must somehow have been designed for our good? This conviction is why the belief in Providence still holds on.

3 GOD'S OVERRULING PROVIDENCE

It holds on too because there is another way of understanding the adverse happenings that sometimes fall to our lot. If we cannot bring ourselves to think that God deliberately brought them about, then the alternative is that human beings in their proud independence – so real, even God-given, that they can deny even God's existence – must be responsible. Either God sent the evil or man sent the evil. But there is a third way to understand this hideously stark alternative: God lets man 'do his damnedest', if he so will, and God will not cancel his independence for the sake of maintaining his sovereignty. No, he will use his power *to bring good out of the evil.* The man in the hospital bed of whom I spoke a moment ago had an inkling of this when he said to the chaplain 'Maybe this has all happened for some good purpose'.

Let me illustrate this with a story from chapter 45 of the book of Genesis. Joseph had eleven brothers and they treated him shamefully, indeed cruelly because he was the youngest in the family and doted on by the father. They caught him in the desert and pushed him down into a dried-out water pit either to die there or to be picked up by any group of merchants who might be trekking across the desert on their way down into Egypt. They couldn't care less what happened to him. Then they had an idea: they could sell the boy to some group of passing merchants. So Joseph found himself a slave in Egypt. He endured many hardships but on account of his striking intelligence and equally striking presence he rose into astonishing prominence in Egypt becoming the first minister in the land of the Pharaoh. Meanwhile, the eleven callous brothers who had pushed him into the pit struggled in famine conditions back in Canaan their homeland. But there was corn in Egypt for sale due to the economic policies of Joseph, their brother, and the brothers went down there from Canaan to buy and were brought before Joseph but did not recognize him in his now semi-regal state. Indeed they were afraid of him and what would become of them. But Joseph said – and these are the words I would have you notice (Genesis 45.4–8):

> So Joseph said to his brothers, 'Come near to me, I pray you . . . I am your brother, Joseph, whom you sold into Egypt. And now do not be distressed, or angry with yourselves, because you sold me here; for God sent me before you to preserve life. For the famine has been in the land these two years; and there are yet five years in which there will be neither ploughing nor harvest. And God sent me before you to preserve for you a remnant on earth, and to keep alive for you many survivors. So it was not you who sent me here, but God; and he has made me a father to Pharaoh, and lord of all his house and ruler over all the land of Egypt.'

End of story; but don't miss the message it contains. The brothers wrought a thoroughly bad, even cruel deed against Joseph but God exercised his sovereignty not to crush the brothers for their evil actions but to bring good out of what they had done. This is Providence in action. This is how God is sovereign ruler of his creation, not to stamp out the freedom of the human race, but to use it for his purposes.

And this is the principle that operated in the crucifixion of Jesus. God did not stamp out this nefarious deed even while it still existed only in the minds and intentions of the perpetrators, he let it run its awful, terrifying course. Jesus died under their torture. But God used that evil to bring about his salvation for the whole world. He made 'the wrath of man to turn to his praise'. This was Providence at work.

Yes, there are problems in plenty about the whole concept of Divine Providence, and when we have said all and thought, never more deeply than at this point in the human story, we have to concede that it is a mystery, a huge paradox; and even if we could encompass it in our minds, it would not be God we were encompassing. God cannot be encompassed by the human mind. But the striking things that happen in our experience from time to time, and which we call coincidences, are not to be denied. They push us to hold on to the truth of Divine Providence, and when we are in doubt we should look again at the cross of our Lord Jesus Christ. God can make even evil acts minister to his purpose of love for all mankind. God is sovereign, but we still have our freedom.

21

THE DISCIPLINE OF SUFFERING

. . . the Lord disciplines those whom he loves.

HEBREWS 12.6 (NEB)

My subject today is pain and suffering. No one will be so foolish as to switch off as if this were a theoretical subject way out from the experience of most of us. We know only too well what it means; and if we haven't as yet felt it we have certainly seen it, sometimes close at hand, frequently in recent years in the pictures on the television screens of heaps and heaps of the ghastly casualties of war. Pain and suffering are universal and consequently are reckoned as an affront to any form of belief in a good God. Surely, so the argument runs, 'if God were good he would wish to make his creatures perfectly happy; if he were almighty he would be able to do what he wished. Therefore God lacks either goodness or power or both, in which case the very idea of God is worthless.'

Let me put it to you. How is it that belief in God comes to be at all? Could it be that there was once a time when 'everything in the garden was lovely', so lovely that people decided there must be a God? Far from it, belief in God arose, developed and kept hold in a world where, as someone has said, there was no chloroform. No, pain does not, without more ado, rub out belief in God. Perhaps we reckon it should, but it doesn't and it hasn't. So we have to come to terms with pain as a regular constituent of the world God has created, apparently it is part of the life he has given us. No wonder that every now and again we want to cry out: why? O God why?

1 RETHINKING OMNIPOTENCE

Perhaps then God isn't omnipotent. Perhaps like all of us God is limited in a network of multifarious cause and effects. This is how the pagans thought and think of their gods: they are really only enlarged variants of ourselves. But we reject this. Fallible gods are not God. Perhaps then we need to revise our idea of omnipotence. We shall have to see that omnipotence does not mean that God can do everything. He can't. He can't for instance make a round square. And if a man has been clouted with a rifle butt God cannot prevent his skull from cracking, though he might with a miracle heal him after it has been cracked. So I recommend that we think of omnipotence, not as the power to do all things, but as the power to make all things serve his purpose, even calamities, even accidents, yes and pain and suffering. The cross of Christ is the supreme example.

And now this. God is limited by his creation. If some parts of his creation are to operate, other parts are ruled out. If you are to have roses in your garden you cannot have large overhanging trees. And if it was God's purpose to create human beings that were free to develop their distinctive individuality, and clearly it was and is, then they cannot be tied on a string to him. They must be independent, able to choose what they will do and what they will be, and this requires a fixed structure of nature where that freedom can be exercised. Nature therefore must follow its own laws regardless of what effects it may have on us. The snow drifting down must go its own way regardless, although it may be a delight to the skier and a deadly hazard to the motorist, making possible a fatal road accident. This is the point I am making. Because God wanted free independent human beings – and we cannot think of any other kind of human being – he had to create a world in which they were able to make choices, and for that to be, the world or the natural order had to abide by fixed laws which could make for pleasure in some situations but also for pain in other situations.

A few days ago a friend came to visit me, bringing her dog. It was a cold day and she had motored a long way, so I lit a fire. On entering the room the dog saw it at once and went and stretched itself at full length in front of it. (I hasten to add, my friend had brought a rug for it to lie on to save my carpet being sprinkled with hairs.) The dog loved the soothing warmth of the fire but the same fire would have inflicted misery on the dog if she lay too close. The same fire would be the provider of pleasure and the provider of pain. Such is the nature of fire.

Do not miss the point I am making. God is limited by the world he has made because his purpose was to create free, independent human beings. What all this means is that if we are to find our way in a world where there is the disturbing, sometimes shattering, presence of pain and suffering we shall need *as a preliminary* the wisdom to accept the world as it is, accept it as God's creation made so in his wisdom, and, as I shall say in a moment, in his purpose of love. Resentment about the world as it is will get us nowhere.

2 SOME PRACTICAL ADVICE

Some of you, perhaps many, may find this kind of abstract reasoning arid, not what you expect from a sermon, so let me turn now and preach as a pastor. First, something simple and straightforward, but which nevertheless must be said. Never entertain the notion that all pain and suffering is the consequence of sin. This is not so. Some of the noblest saints have suffered terribly, indeed their sufferings contributed to their sainthood. So rub out the question if and when it begins to form in your mind, 'What have I done to deserve this?' It does not apply. And God does not send pain as a punishment.

And secondly this. Do not think that pain can expiate sin. It cannot. And do not play with the idea of deliberately inflicting pain on oneself in order to make oneself a better man or woman. I know there is a tradition of this form of harsh asceticism, but there is nothing to support it in the teaching of Christ.

Do not imagine that the infliction of pain on those guilty of some form of criminal activity will automatically make them better persons. It may make them worse. What pain and suffering do to a person is conditioned by the way they bear it. Pain may ennoble. It may coarsen. The most outstanding example of this can be seen in the lives of those who have faced the most horrible experiences in warfare.

Now let me move a little nearer home and the more ordinary experiences of pain and suffering some of us know only too well. What they offer us is not the grounds for complaining about God and the way he has made the world but *an opportunity for heroism*. I have seen old ladies crippled with arthritis unable even to operate an electric light switch, but yet remaining consistently cheerful. That is heroic. And if sometimes the faces of the elderly appear somewhat grim, it may not be because they are bad-tempered but because they have tried, and are trying, their best to resist pain. It is the constant nagging pain that is the hardest to bear, the kind of hot searing pain that inhibits even speech, let alone grumbling.

3 LOVE INVOLVES DISCIPLINE

And now my last point in this sermon, in some ways the most difficult to accept, but it is the message of my text from Hebrews 12.6, 'the Lord disciplines those whom he loves'. We don't for the most part like discipline. Verse 11 of this chapter of the letter to the Hebrews says this plainly. 'Discipline, no doubt, is never pleasant; at the time it seems painful, but in the end it yields for those who have been trained by it the peaceful harvest of an honest life.' Jesus taught this to his disciples in picture language the night before he was crucified. He said 'I am the real vine and my Father is the gardener. Every barren branch of mine he cuts away; and every fruiting branch he cleans, to make it more fruitful still . . . This is my Father's story, that you may bear fruit in plenty and so be my disciples. As the Father has loved me, so I have loved you.' There is no such person as a gardener without secateurs, probably kept constantly handy in his pocket. To have flowers there has to be the discipline of cutting back. And the cutting back is only done to the plants he cares about and values.

Let me remind you of the dog my friend brought when she came to see me. It was a lovely animal, so welcoming, so friendly. My friend obviously loved this creature and it was plain the dog loved her. She loved her from the moment she saw her in the kennels and decided to buy her, but she needed much disciplining, cleaning up, brushing and being made obedient. And she received this discipline. She was sent to a dog school, and no doubt found it painful. But her mistress sent her *because she loved* her, and when she had undergone the strict training, her mistress loved her all the more, and I am not surprised, for she really was a most attractive animal when I saw her, not only to look at but in her response to people.

Need I press my point further? 'The Lord disciplines those whom he loves' (Hebrews 12.6). What a long way this is from thinking of pain and suffering as the indication that God is angry with us! Pain and suffering may operate as a form of discipline the result of which is to make us more attractive people. Perhaps we can begin to understand and accept this a little if we reflect on the reverse, the man or woman who is perpetually grumbling and fighting about what has befallen them. Such a person is not attractive. The instinctive reaction is to give them a wide berth. I am not saying all this is easy – I know a little bit about pain and suffering – but if we can lay hold of the truth that God loves us there will be gains from what at times we have to undergo. Let me remind you of my text, 'the Lord disciplines those whom he loves' (Hebrews 12.6). Never lose hold of the love of God for us even when the pain and suffering are hard to bear.

22

DWELLING IN CHRIST

I am the vine, and you the branches. He who dwells in me, as I dwell in him, bears much fruit; for apart from me you can do nothing.

JOHN 15.5 (NEB)

In my sermon today I want to clear up any possible misunderstanding. I may have given the impression, I hope not, but I may have given the impression that being a Christian is essentially thinking rightly about God, Christ, the Holy Spirit and similar basic beliefs, we might call them doctrines, and the point of preaching is to correct erroneous ideas. This would make Christianity equivalent to orthodoxy, that is to say if we think correctly about these doctrines we shall be Christians, proper Christians. This is not so and nothing could have been further from my mind in preaching these sermons under the general title *Preaching What We Believe*. What has concerned me is to help clear away, if I could, some of the apparent current uncertainty about what we believe, and some of the consequent stumbling blocks that make Christian belief difficult for some people. Perhaps this could be called an elementary exercise in 'apologetics'. Not that I reckon apologetics a substitute for proclaiming the Gospel, but they have a proper place and that is to prepare the ground for evangelism. The fact is some people find Christian belief difficult intellectually, perhaps we all do at times. This does not necessarily indicate an unwillingness to believe, but an inability to believe coupled maybe with a longing to believe. The preacher has to meet this situation and at a level ordinary people can grasp.

1 WHAT IS BEING A CHRISTIAN?

In this sermon however I wish to go beyond apologetics. I have said Christianity is not in its essence right thinking about our beliefs, in other words orthodoxy. What then is it? What is being a Christian? This is the subject of this sermon, and if its character and style is different from its predecessors in this collection, being more like a commentary on a passage of Scripture, my defence is that the subject requires it.

The passage of Scripture we shall consider, John, chapter 15, has a dramatic setting. The twelve disciples were together with Jesus in an upper room in Jerusalem. They were uneasy, sensing the hostility building up against their Master outside. What shook them to the depths was Jesus' announcement that an insider, one of the twelve in that very room, would betray his whereabouts to the enemy so that they could arrest him. They couldn't believe it, not when they saw Judas receive the bread dipped in the dish by Jesus, the host at the meal, and handed to him. But they watched him leave the table, open the door, and go out into the night. He did not come back.

Jesus continued the conversation at the table and this is what he said. 'I shall not talk much longer with you for the Prince of this world approaches. He has no rights over me, but the world must be shown that I love the Father and do exactly as he commands; so up, let us go forward!' As they went their way they passed the great golden vine that trailed over the Temple porch lit up at night by the full moon. It was regarded as a symbol of the nation of Israel, its calling by God and also its unfaithfulness. Doubtless looking at it, Jesus said 'I am the true vine', and then, turning to the disciples, 'I am the vine, you are the branches. He who dwells in me, as I dwell in him, bears much fruit; for apart from me you can do nothing.'

So now from out of this dramatic scene comes the answer to our question 'What is being a Christian?' It is *dwelling in Christ* like a branch of a vigorous fruit-bearing vine for whom the gardener cares, it belongs to the vine, it is part of it and as such flourishes, not only attractive but valuable for the grapes it bears. A Christian is the man or woman who dwells in Christ, everything else is peripheral: race, class, income group, trade, profession, education, language, the essential is to dwell in Christ. This is the heart of Christianity. This is what it means to be a Christian.

But I fancy I can hear someone commenting: this is all very well, but how does one dwell in Christ in practice? What must one do? How does one start?

2 FAITH IN RESPONSE TO GOD'S INITIATIVE

First, let me say this: not by trying to copy Christ. No one is able to imitate another and be authentic. Each one of us is an individual with unrepeatable characteristics, potentialities and limitations. We have to be 'our own man', 'our own woman', to use a modern catch-phrase. We come to be dwelling in Christ therefore not by struggling to copy him but in the first place by believing in him. That is where we start. And this belief, this faith, is not in the very first place the outcome of an intellectual exercise, weighing up the information we have about Christ, so far as it goes, and then deciding for him, accounting our allegiance a risk worth taking. This may or may not come later. No, faith in the first place and in the last place is *response*, that is the key word for the key action, response, saying 'Yes' to the approach of God to us, for he is the one who takes the initiative.

How God approaches us will vary in a thousand ways. It may be by means of a scene in nature of breathtaking beauty, so wonderful we cannot find words to describe it. It may be a mother taking her newborn baby in her arms for the first time. Don't tell me nothing could be further from her thoughts at that wonderful moment than God! Or maybe the thought of Providence acting for us when a job turned up after weeks of fruitless search; or when we struggled to our feet again after a crippling illness. Yes, I know God may approach us dramatically in a mighty sermon or a stirring evangelistic campaign, or even a theological lecture! But God comes close to most people in the ordinary events of ordinary living, he comes, as it were, stealing into our garden. Half baffled, we pass it off with some such lame expression as 'I had a funny feeling', but in the secret of our hearts it really constitutes our response to something like a faith 'Yes'; if so, that is the beginning of faith, it is the first step of dwelling in Christ, probably a timid teetering step.

But intellect has soon to come in, otherwise our faith is mere credulity, a flabby thing without backbone; we have to think through our experience and apply our reason, then we have faith proper. The truth still stands however: the initiative in the first place came from God. So Jesus' words in John, chapter 15 to his disciples, 'You did not choose me: I chose you'.

But 'dwelling in Christ' obviously means more than this initial response of faith to the approach of God to us whatever way that approach may have taken. It means *living* in the consciousness of Christ's presence. Christ as our support and succour, Christ as our friend when so much in life seems to be against us, Christ as a guide when we are in doubt which is the right course of action to follow, Christ as our judge but at the same time as our Saviour, Christ taking our arm as it were when we feel we can struggle no longer. To some people, perhaps to many, this may sound like unrealistic pious talk. There come times however in our experience when the bottom seems to have fallen out of life. We wonder how we shall 'get through' (as we say). Bereavement is one such time, especially sudden bereavement. But we did get through. We came out of the tunnel. And if during those days of darkness we found it hard to pray, we learned afterwards that many people had been praying for us: 'O Lord, support us all the day long of this troublous life . . .' We were supported; 'dwelling in Christ' means this and much more.

3 THE RESULT OF THIS INDWELLING

And now something even more important than our initial faith and our continuing spiritual experience. There is what this chapter 15 of St John's gospel calls the fruit of our dwelling in Christ. Listen to the words again: 'You did not choose me: I chose you and appointed you to go on bearing fruit, fruit that shall last.' It is for the fruit that a gardener plans and cares for the tree, not simply for its attractive foliage and blossom. It is the grapes he looks for, glossy grapes, sweet to the taste, not hard and bitter, indispensable for the production of full-bodied wine, but there will be no such fruit unless the tree is consistently cared for and fed. So it is with being a Christian. Dwelling in Christ requires sustaining. It is a rough world in which we live. The rush, the scramble, the frustrations and the worries of modern life can so easily squeeze anything like 'dwelling in Christ' out of existence. So we must look to the supports and defences that do exist.

There is the Church, the fellowship of other Christians. It is well-nigh impossible to continue dwelling in Christ if one is alone. We need to meet with other Christians, meet with them when they gather together in prayer and worship, including, it is hoped, singing. Without this fellowship our dwelling in Christ is likely to be diminished like a tree in the orchard not supported in its early stage of growth by strong stakes and always thereafter cared for and pruned. In default of this nurture there will result a stunted, even shrivelled tree, and any harvest of grapes minimal.

There is also Bible reading. In order to continue dwelling in Christ it is necessary to feed on the Word of God. The Bible becomes the Word of God when we read it with expectancy. Scholarship has its part to play but is secondary. We need to come to it to nourish our dwelling in Christ, and this means regularly coming, regular reading. Food would do little for the bodily health and strength of the partaker if only taken now and again. Bible Reading Fellowships are of real value, especially when groups of readers gather together from time to time to discuss and share what they are reading.

And there are the Sacraments, especially the Holy Communion. There we feed on the Body and Blood of Christ, there we are nourished by communion, communion with Christ and communion with one another. Our dwelling in Christ will continue if we come regularly to receive the spiritual food offered to us in the Sacrament which the Church has ministered throughout the centuries in obedience to the words of Jesus in the Upper Room in Jerusalem the night before his crucifixion when he broke bread and poured out wine: 'This is my body. This is my blood. Do this in remembrance of me.'

Our dwelling in Christ then needs nourishment and care, if it is to bear fruit. 'You did not choose me: I chose you and appointed you to go on bearing fruit, fruit that shall last.' And this also from the fifteenth chapter of John: 'I am the vine, and you the branches. He who dwells in me, as I dwell in him, bears much fruit; for apart from me you can do nothing.' So the words of Jesus in that upper room as John has recorded and expounded them.

But what is the fruit? It is good works. It is action, practical action. It is a different and distinctive way of life, noticeable, perhaps even striking. It is love of our fellow men and women, yes even if they are our enemies. 'By this shall all men know that you are my disciples if you love one another' (John 13.35).

Do not therefore make the mistake of counting 'dwelling in Christ' a private personal, pious disposition and nothing more. Where it is genuine, where it is real, it shows itself in an openness to people, a concern for them and a readiness to do what is possible to help them when help is required. A man, a woman dwelling in Christ is never standoffish, never conceited, boastful or rude, never quick to take offence but patient and ready to give the benefit of the doubt, and takes no enjoyment whatsoever from other people's sins. Say 'yes' then to God's approach to you however it comes and nourish the indwelling of his Spirit. The experience makes new men and women, not all alike, far from it, but notable for one thing in common, love of one another.

23

LIFE AFTER DEATH

For he has broken the power of death and brought life and immortality to light through the Gospel.

2 TIMOTHY 1.10 (NEB)

In this series of sermons entitled *Preaching What We Believe* the subject 'Life after death' could hardly be left out. In the Apostles' Creed recited at Morning and Evening prayer there is this confession: 'I believe . . . in the resurrection of the body and the life everlasting', and at the Holy Communion: 'We look for the resurrection of the dead and the life of the world to come.' Could anything be more clear? This is what we believe, and as I see it, this is what we should preach.

1 BELIEF IN IMMORTALITY BEFORE CHRIST

So let me go back to my text. 'For he (Christ) has broken the power of death and brought life and immortality to light through the Gospel.' Please listen carefully. Life after death was not a new idea which Christianity proclaimed; three thousand years before Christ the Egyptians were fascinated by it. They could scarcely let it out of their minds. Think of those pyramids, still among the wonders of the world. How on earth were they constructed out there in the desert? But more tantalizing still: why were they constructed? It was to provide for the Pharaohs after their deaths which, it was believed, their souls survived; and so food, drink and other necessities of life were placed in these giant tombs within reach of the embalmed bodies. Why exactly it was thought necessary for the body if it was the soul that survived death is a puzzle. What is clear however is that the Egyptians believed in an immortality of some kind.

And now the other great civilization, the Babylonian. There too a belief in immortality held sway. It was a gloomy belief. The dead were thought to live in a vast underworld which the light of day never penetrated; they fed on dust and were guarded by demons. There were no distinctions; there was neither heaven nor hell, and no way of escape. What is clear is that the Babylonians, centuries before Christ, a highly civilized people, did not reckon that 'when you were dead you were done for', though considering the gloomy prospect of the underworld, annihilation might have seemed preferable, but it was not contemplated and it was unthinkable.

The next great ancient civilization, the Greek, reckoned that the dead were, as it were, only half dead. The body was a kind of prison and when death came the soul escaped because it is immortal and has an affinity with God. Good souls will pass to the islands of the blessed, guilty souls will pay the price of their evil deeds. This thinking was a considerable advance on what went before, reaching perhaps its height in the thought of the famous philosopher Plato who saw the present life as a preparation for the next; if worthy, it led to a final rest in God.

The Romans, a very practical down-to-earth people, nourished a kind of belief in immortality in which reverence for 'the shades', as they called them, of their ancestors played the most prominent part. Scepticism however began to grow among the intelligentsia, and because it provided so little in the way of hope, attention began to be turned to Eastern religions, especially Mithraism, taking a hold, in particular among the soldiers, but it was all vague and uncertain.

I am sorry if all this has sounded rather like a lesson in ancient history but I have gone over the ground in order to light up my text. 'For he (Christ) has broken the power of death and brought life and immortality to light through the Gospel.' The belief in immortality was there before Christ came, but there was little hope in it and no joy. What Christ did was to bring that very gloomy belief out into the light, and he did it by being raised from the dead himself on Easter Day, something completely new and making for a gospel, that is, a proclamation of good news. Listen to the text again. 'He (Christ) has broken the power of death and brought life and immortality to light through the Gospel.'

2 CHRISTIAN BELIEF ABOUT LIFE AFTER DEATH

But what happens at death? What is the life after death? Certainly not the gloomy half-existence in a dark underworld as the civilizations before Christ thought. We believe in heaven, not a place of disembodied spirits moving around in a kind of semi-existence, but of vital resurrected individuals, vital because they have eternal life. What is more, each soul is given a resurrection body, a new body, a body to become the vehicle of the life of the individual soul which survives death. Even as our physical bodies on earth are the means of expressing what we are, that is what our souls or spirits are making for the real person.

Now of course we can turn a deaf ear to all this and cry out 'Ah, but you can't prove it'. No, and if we have no use for the Bible there is nothing to be said on the life after death, although recently claims have been made for belief in life after death on the basis of the testimony of those who have survived what is called 'clinical death'. This however is an area of investigation which has not so far produced generally accepted answers that are convincing.

So we return to the Scriptures. Here are some of the lights they provide. Life in heaven will not be mere everlastingness. According to the teaching of Jesus there will be work to do and joy in doing it. And there will be no personal misfits in heaven. Let me quote the words of Jesus as we have heard them in the Authorized Verison of St John, chapter 14: 'In my Father's house are many mansions.' 'Dwelling places' would be a better rendering as in the New English Bible. 'I go to prepare a place for you.' If that place is thought of as a lock, each individual is the key which exactly fits, and because it fits it can perform its true function, the function proper to it. To put the matter another way, each one of us will be at home in heaven. Our individuality will find its complete justification. One of the facts about human beings that has always amazed me is that for all the millions and millions that exist, and presumably have existed, there are no two persons exactly alike. We are all different down to our fingerprints. Is this accidental or is it part of the design of the Creator? It seems to me to be crying aloud that each one of us is valuable for himself/herself alone. And if in the life of the here and now, many of us, perhaps most of us have never been appreciated for what we are, in heaven that will no longer be the case. 'In my Father's house are many mansions.' 'I go to prepare *a place for you.*' So the words of Jesus, according to St John's gospel, the night before he passed to the heavenly place himself.

So we believe in heaven. Of course the subject often is made a mockery, 'pie in the sky when you die'. It will certainly not be a belief to be referred to at a political meeting because of the widespread – and I may add erroneous – idea that those who believe in heaven will show little or no concern for improving the living conditions of people in this world. Without a belief in life after death however we are a people without hope, and this is the road to meaninglessness and ineffectiveness, a state of affairs we hardly dare face. Is it not then the duty of the Christian Church to preach what we believe, even if at times we are mocked for it? There is life after death, and heaven does await us.

But what about hell? Do we believe in this? I don't want to, and I don't believe in it if it means suffering for ever and ever, ever in physical torment. It does not square with a God of love. And yet I cannot think that those individuals of whom we have known that they have given themselves to monumental cruelty, knowing better, will suffer no loss, irrevocable loss, for this would be a travesty of justice. Perhaps hell is the ultimate realization that the bliss which could be theirs is gone for them for ever. Hell is the realm of nothingness. Of course we wish to avoid this subject of hell. I wish to avoid it, but it is there in the teaching of Jesus: Luke 16.22 and Matthew 25.46.

3 THE BEDROCK OF OUR FAITH

I come back to my text, 2 Timothy 1.10: 'For he (Christ) has broken the power of death and brought life and immortality to light through the Gospel.' This is where we need to anchor our faith and our thoughts. There is much about the life after death we cannot understand but the resurrection of Christ stands as a beacon light. The grave is not the end, he rose from it and we shall rise. Christianity is built on this and it says: do not be afraid. Our future is assured and not a gloomy one but full of radiant joy and accomplishment. This is what we believe. This is what we preach. I plead with you to rest your souls in this faith.

24
OTHER RELIGIONS

The real light which enlightens every man was even then coming into the world.

JOHN 1.9 (NEB)

Hardly a week goes by without our being told by the news media that in Britain today we have a multiracial society. This is not accurate. What we have is a British society in which there are an increasing number of racial minorities each with their own language, customs and, to some extent, religious beliefs. This however poses problems, not least in our schools. When I was a boy, school assembly consisted every morning of a simple act of Christian worship. This picture makes little sense today where a large percentage of the children may belong to an ethnic group whose religion is other than Christian. In such situations there had better be the assembly without the worship. But what about Religious Education? Is this to be dropped as well? Or is what is called Comparative Religion to be taught with the aim of inculcating respect for all religions, which is indeed desirable and laudable? But does this mean that all religions are 'much of a muchness', all are but different roads making for the same destination? What do we believe about this? What do we preach? This is my subject for this sermon.

1 THE *LOGOS*

I want to start from my text, John 1.9: 'The real light which enlightens every man was even then coming into the world', that is in the time when John the Baptist was conducting his ministry down by the river Jordan, possibly about the year

AD 28. But the light did not only begin to shine then, it has shone since the world began. What John was writing about was the Word (capital W) of God, that is, God's creative Word, the *Logos* through whom all things came to be, all alive with his life, and that life the light of men, indeed it enlightens every human being who is, or whoever has been in the world. What a statement! Its breadth almost takes our breath away – every human being! And as if that is not staggering enough, in due time that creative Word, that *Logos*, actually came into this world, our world. He is the one we know as Jesus Christ. Can we believe this? Do we believe it? If we do, we cannot possibly nurse a narrow, racial view of our Christian religion. Let me quote my text again from John 1.9, this time in the words of the Authorized Version of the Bible: 'That was the true Light, which *lighteth every man* that cometh into the world.'

Now it follows from this that before Christ came people lived by the light they experienced, however dimly. They did not invent the light, it was their response to the divine light, a response which was expressed and fed by disparate local customs, cultures and languages. And the situation is similar after Christ came in those parts of the world where his name is virtually unknown. The people lived by such light as they had and so religions grew up, non-Christian religions, but they are not therefore utterly destitute of the truth. There is light in them, 'the real light, the true light, which enlightens every man'. Christians must never write them off, never despise them, never underrate them, for to do so would be to reject aspects of ultimate truth. This is not hard to see in the great religions like Judaism, Islam and Buddhism, to give only three obvious examples.

But this does not make all religions the same. Because some Christians have not understood this, they have thought their own faith threatened by this openness. This is not so. The distinctive truth of the Christian religion is the Incarnation: 'the Word became flesh; he came to dwell among us, and we saw his glory, such glory as befits the Father's only Son, full of grace and truth' (John 1.14 NEB). The light of life we see in Christ, far from blinding us to the truth that is in religions other than the Christian, enables us to recognize it when we see it and count it authentic. Nor is there any ground for Christians to adopt a superior stance. Christ, Light of the World though he was, was never superior. He was lowly, he was open to all. He warmed to people whoever they were, he in fact loved them. The attitude proper to Christians is one of humble gratitude for the gift, yes gift, of being able to see Christ as the Light of the World by which light we can recognize light wherever it shines and in whatever form or religion, even though frequently blurred. The Christian's confidence should be so securely based in the Incarnation, *which is unique*, that he/she can be open to truth wherever it is found, the very opposite of narrowness.

And this understanding has an internal message for the Christian Church. Sectarianism and party divisions do not square with the breadth of the truth as it is presented in the gospel of the Incarnation. Differences of emphasis there must be, different ways of perceiving the truth of Christ, for we are all different and see what we see from different angles; and to be true to ourselves we must stand by what we see, but not discredit those who see differently. As St Paul wrote to the Christians at Rome (12.18 RSV), 'If possible, so far as it depends upon you, live peaceably with all'. In our situation, Catholic with Protestant and Protestant with Catholic.

2 A COMIC STORY WITH A SERIOUS MESSAGE

Let me end with a story about God's openness and care for all, even outsiders, so outside as to be reckoned beyond the pale. It comes from the literature of that people who stood more aloof than any nation from their neighbours: I refer to the Jews. It is a story commonly misunderstood, the story of Jonah. About all that people in general know about Jonah, if they know anything, is that he is said in the Bible story to have been swallowed by a great fish (a whale?) and vomited up on dry land to continue his life work, just as if he could. What readers generally fail to grasp is that the writer of Jonah was seeking to gain a hearing for a truth which unless pitched in a half-comic form would be met with closed ears. It was the truth that God cares about outsiders, even Assyrians, even the people of Nineveh whom every Jew hated.

Here then is the story. Jonah, charged by God to call Nineveh to repent of its wickedness, rebelled and paid for a passage on a ship travelling west, not east, as far from Nineveh as possible. But God hurled a great wind on the sea so that the ship threatened to break up, whereupon the fearful crew prayed each to his god; but not Jonah, the true Israelite. He descended to the hold and fell asleep. The captain, finding him, sharply reproved him for not praying to his god to save them. And when he heard from Jonah's own lips that he was a Hebrew, a fearer of the God of heaven, maker of sea and dry land, the anxiety of the whole crew increased mightily; whereupon Jonah bade them cast him into the sea in order to still its continued raging. But heathen though they were they had compassion and attempted to row the ship back to land; but in vain. So casting themselves on God's mercy they tossed Jonah into the water. God however had a great fish ready to swallow up Jonah and he was in its belly for three days and three nights.

And now the climax. Vomited out upon dry land, Jonah heard God's command a second time: 'Go to Nineveh and preach what I tell you.' It was a grim message but he delivered it. 'Yet forty days, and Nineveh shall be overthrown.' But it wasn't overthrown. The Ninevites believed God and repented, they repented from the king downwards. They put on sackcloth. Even the animals were clothed in sackcloth. Jonah was furious. He felt this reprieve for Nineveh made him look silly. He as good as told God so in a hopeless prayer. 'Is this not what I said when I was yet in my country? That is why I made haste to flee to Tarshish.' And then these words, the key to the story: 'for I knew that thou art a gracious God and merciful, slow to anger, and abounding in steadfast love, and repentest of evil.' It was too much for Jonah. 'Therefore now, O Lord, take my life from me; for it is better for me to die than to live.' He couldn't suffer this openness.

But he didn't die. He went and sat outside Nineveh to see

what would become of it. And now the bit in the story even more comic than the big fish swallowing Jonah. He was hot out there in the glaring sunshine, so God made a plant grow to give him shade, but then a worm to kill it. Jonah was sick of God's tactics, as well he might be, and repeated his refrain, 'It is better for me to die than to live'. And now the punch-line in the story in the form of a question, just as Jesus on occasions used to drive home his message: 'Jonah, you pity the plant, and should not I pity Nineveh, that great city in which there are more than a hundred and twenty thousand persons who do not know their right hand from their left, and also much cattle?' . . . Curtain.

And when we don't know whether to laugh or cry over such a comic tale the word of God begins to bite. Exclusive religion which shuts out the ignorant masses is not God's way, and when we try and behave as if it is, we make ourselves look silly. We need to be open to all, whoever they are and whatever they have done or not done. I come back to my text from St John's gospel. 'The real light which enlightens every man was even then coming into the world.' With such a belief, how can we possibly be exclusive in our approach to people, how can we not recognize the light where it is shining and how it is shining in religions other than our own, even when it is dim or blurred?